Wong Kar-wai.

D1599870

Chicago Public Library

REFERENCE

Form 178 rev. 1-94

editor assistant: Stéphane Argillet

Special Thanks to:
Jacky Pang, Norman Wang, Marjan van der Haar (Fortissimo)
Alban Barré, Yannick Haennel, Élisabeth Lagane, Nadia Tazi, Cathy Lenihan,
HK Orient Extrême Cinéma.

© Editions Dis Voir
3, rue Beautreillis
75004 Paris
ISBN 2-906571-67-9

© Jet Tone Production for all the pictures used in this book

PRINTED IN EUROPE

WONG KAR WAI

WONG KAR WAI

JEAN- MARC LALANNE

DAVID MARTINEZ

ACKBAR ABBAS

JIMMY NGAI

Ouvrage aidé par le Ministère français chargé de la Culture

Heaps of Story. There is a short story by Borges in which cartographers set out to draw up a map of the Empire which would take all its tiniest particularities into account. No pathway, no clearing, not the slightest pile of pebbles was to be overlooked. Little by little, with such utter attention to detail, the map grew vastly out of proportion until it exactly covered the very territory it was intended to denote. Unusable, it began to disintegrate where it lay and only a few remaining shreds were ever found, scattered in the desert. Wong Kar-wai's films resemble this map, dreamed too big to hold together in one piece and of which there remains only bits and pieces. Initially, *As Tears Go By* was intended as the first part of a urban crime trilogy. But the next two parts never happened. *Days of Being Wild* is the first part of a large diptych which remains unfinished. *Chungking Express* was to include three other stories, but ended up with only two. *Ashes of Time* exists in versions of various lengths. *Fallen Angels* can at once be thought of as one of the episodes intended for *Chungking Express* and as a possible follow-up to *As Tears Go By*. Finally, *Happy Together* was initially conceived as a three hour film, but which the film-maker chose to cut to only an hour and a half to show at Cannes. Wong Kar-wai's filmography is frayed at the edges, each work the column of an unbuilt temple. In this way, each film is a sort of fallen angel, which has tumbled from the celestial realm of the work as it was initially imagined.

This incompleteness should not be seen as a mere failure to carry them through to the end. His whole aesthetic project is based on the openness of the work. Each film is to be seen as a fragment, as is exemplified in the finale of *Days of Being Wild*. Mimi (Carina Lau) arrives in the Philippines in the hope of finding Yuddi (Leslie Chung). A narrative track is sketched out, which the film, already at an end, will have to leave undeveloped. Then there appears a character we have never seen (played by Tony Leung). He's in his room, getting ready to go out. He gets dressed, meticulously smoothes down his hair, looks at himself in the mirror, all with a perfectionism reminiscent of Yuddi's mania for elegance. One clearly takes up the torch from the other, and we realize that the story could go on with this new hero. The film then finishes with a first scene, that of the second film of the abandoned diptych. For the viewer who knows nothing of the initial project, this enigmatic epilogue is rather perplexing. Like suspension points at the end of a sentence, it leaves traces in the film itself of how profoundly unfinished it is, stigmata of what it might have been but will not be. This extra piece takes meaning away rather than adding more; its value is first of all as a clue to all the missing pieces.

This narrative jolt is only the most spectacular example of a more general aesthetic project which consists in favoring detail above totality, and the part above the whole. Wong Kar-wai's narratives are always made up of pieces that never add up to a full set. Sometimes the different narrative parts are simply juxtaposed (*Chunking Express* is a film made up of sketches), and sometimes they are interwoven in a more convoluted way (*Fallen Angels, Days of Being Wild*). In their interlacing night-time city itineraries, the characters incessantly cross one another's paths. The driving principle of his fiction consists in forming pairs (there are really very few group scenes in Wong Kar-wai's work, the characters are always in groups of two) and the film continues until all the possibilities for pairing up the characters have been exhausted. *Days of Being Wild* very rigorously goes through all combinations of two possible. In the same way, in *Fallen Angels* the pairs change according to circumstance and chance meetings. But these entwined stories don't follow one another with the metronomic rhythm of *Short Cuts* (where each couple is allotted their scene one after the other). They always move forward haphazardly, and for twenty or so minutes, characters we thought of as secondary come to the fore, during which time we practically forget about the main characters. The narrative's perspective lines are constantly undone, only to be put back together more sinuously than ever. Every fragment of the story stages a temporary overthrow inside the film.

Ashes of Time is, from this point of view, the author's most complex film. Adopting the sketch form of *Chungking Express* — it is a succession of almost autonomous scenes — while at the same time these scenes are spanned by several main themes which can only be understood at the film's end. Even *As Tears Go By*, probably his simplest and most linear work, includes purely digressive scenes which elude the strictly narrative logic. One example is the young woman who was Andy Lau's mistress and who had an abortion. She is in a scene at the beginning of the film and then disappears. We come across her once again three quarters of the way through the story in the course of a sequence of no dramatic use whatsoever. Andy Lau meets her by chance in the street, she has changed a lot, has married and seems to be blossoming in her new life. The main character suddenly seems to long for a life he never knew, which would have been his had they stayed together and kept the child she got rid of... Through this arbitrary fictional evasion, this break in the story's running, it is the film itself which, like its character, flirts with a fiction it was not to know, and looks over into another film and seems to regret having told the story it did rather than the other. In *If on a winter's night a traveler*, Italo Calvino describes the torments of a writer who is never able to tell a single story. At every turn in his story he imagines a variety of possibilities for the next scene, a variety of different outcomes. Telling a story is always tantamount to killing these various ramifications, narrowing the choice down to only one of them, and he cannot bring himself to sacrifice them; he wants to bring them all into one single text. He dreams of a total fiction comprising all the imaginable developments out of an initial situation. Such that his novel cannot be finished and is lost in the infinity of possibilities. Wong Kar-wai partially fulfills the dream of the writer Calvino. Each of his films bears the traces of another story it could have told and which he couldn't bring himself to do away with. Wong Kar-wai's fiction films are less stories than crossroads of stories.

From the Modern to the Contemporary. This inventiveness in narrative is obviously synchronous with the experimentation of a whole sector of contemporary *cinéma d'auteur* where the quest for new forms is once again bound up with the question of narration. Pascale Ferran's *Petits arrangements avec la mort*, recent films by Atom Egoyan, Kieslowski, *Pulp Fiction*, *Usual Suspects*, *Lost Highway* or the last Téchiné (*Les Voleurs*), to take a selection of films and directors who, having met with a certain echo from critics, all put the question of narrative at the center of their preoccupations. Most of these films, like those of Wong Kar-wai, are based on the pattern of the maze and the jumbling of time series. How is it then that Wong Kar-wai seems to be way ahead of everyone else? Perhaps because his complex work in developing narrative is nothing in comparison with his experimentation with images, one forever short-circuiting the other. As complex and convoluted as his narrative devices are, the *mise en scène* always wins out. His way of

taking images over and treating them like autonomous material, as malleable as clay, Wong Kar-wai has set himself apart as the most contemporary film-maker of the bunch.

This notion of contemporaneousness perhaps marks a new threshold. In the 60's, cinema was modern; then post-modern, or even mannerist. Today, there may be a way of opening a space outside of the great diachronic narratives, and Wong Kar-wai's cinema has plunged into it. Yet his first films fully embrace the aesthetics of modernity, gnawed at as they are by that entirely modern consciousness of *coming after*: after classicism, after its forms had reached total maturity, ie. after they had started to fall to pieces. Henceforth they had to be deconstructed and accompanied in their inexorable decomposition. Wong Kar-wai's first three works are atypical genre films. *As Tears Go By* contorts the rules of the urban crime story, dissolves the dramatic construction (the story is incredibly repetitive, without any real progression) in order to make the characters and their motivations more complex. *Ashes of Time* dismembers the classic sword-fight film and continues Leone's work on the western while pushing it right to its extreme mannerist limit. Moments of latency swell out until they constitute the film's only material. The battle scenes are left out. The characters, almost always filmed from very close up (cf. Leone), spend the whole film waiting, frozen in pretentious and languid postures. In this spectral poem, almost nothing of the ancient society of Heroes and Myths remains; just a few survivors, spread out over the miles of deserts, where the lands are ravaged by drought and the people decimated by sickness. Even Clint Eastwood has never gone as far in twilight imagery and funereal aestheticizing of the rituals of a genre. Finally, *Days of Being Wild* comes across as a reformulation of modern film as a genre, a sort of rereading of Nicholas Ray done by Antonioni. Here again, the film flirts erratically, languidly, with its own unfolding.

In Wong Kar-wai's short filmography, *Chungking Express* already looks like something of a Copernican revolution. It is moreover not without significance that the film was made during a break in the shooting of *Ashes of Time*. With *Chungking Express*, the work Wong Kar-wai had been doing essentially came to a stop, only to soar off in another direction. It is no longer a question of finding one's place in a linear (and Darwinian) progression of film History in order to bring about one's own personal adjustments and contribute one's own ideas. On the contrary, *Chungking Express* like *Fallen Angels* strives to haul cinema out of the cinema, to connect it to different sites, those carrying the large flows of new images, of audio-visual and of virtual reality. To spin out the Borgesian metaphor, the new territories mapped out by Wong Kar-wai are the abstract regions of modern communications; a land of images where cinema's mystique, as an art of registering, would cease to have any meaning, where images would seem self-engendered, deploying themselves without any reference to the real. As a matter of fact, the first shot in Wong Kar-wai's first film is a wall of televisions on which we see moving blue clouds like a monochrome in motion, the promise of a world where everything is already an image and where images no longer refer to anything but abstract forms.

How does the generation and free circulation of images work? In *Days of Being Wild*, after a few preliminary scenes, a long lateral traveling shot comes upon a lush green jungle. The camera looks down on the vegetation; the shot may be from a helicopter. The movement is slow, muffled, as if inviting reverie. There is no way to attribute any significance to this image. The preceding shots, and those which are to follow, show a strictly urban milieu. Where is this jungle? What is it doing at the beginning of this story? Who is looking down on it from so high above? It is also difficult to assign it any metaphorical significance (what is it a metaphor of?). It is a shot, almost superfluous, which rebuffs meaning. At the very end of the film, by which time we have forgotten about it, the same shot comes back. The main character, Udi (Leslie Cheung), is dying on a train. We see the same lush vegetation moving past, but this time a second, broader-angle shot brings a railway bridge into the picture of this junglescape. We are finally able to attribute this sight of a hazy jungle to someone. The trees are thus the last things that registered on Yudi's retina as he lay dying. The lateral traveling corresponds to the train movement, the downward point of view from high above to the bridge the train is crossing. Everything becomes clear. Except the decision to use the shot on two occasions, one of which was right at the beginning of the film. In other words, the image had been shown (by the film) before it was seen (by the character).

6 ▶

8 ▶▶

7 ▶

In *Happy Together* we find another example of an *image shown before having been seen*. In the first sequences, the film's main characters, the couple Fai (Tony Leung) and Po-Wing (Leslie Cheung) are crossing Argentina on their way to the Iguazu Falls. But they get lost and return to Buenos Aires before finishing their trip. Yet the falls appear in the picture. The point of view is from above, once again from an airplane; the shot lasts a long time, bestowing the image with the same coefficient of unreality as the one in *Days of Being Wild*. It is a purely contemplative shot, except we don't know who's contemplating, given that the characters never made it to the falls. At the end of the film, Fai travels to the falls alone, sees them for the first time and we as viewers then see the shot again, this time governed by the character's point of view. Certain images thus have the power to become autonomous and free themselves from any narrative context: they become transparent and float freely on the film's surface.

Wong Kar-wai has worked a great deal on the theme of the last image, the one which returns when everything is finished. In *As Tears Go By*, it is a memory-image which comes to the surface: in a very beautiful linking movement, Andy Lau collapses, hit by a bullet, while almost subliminally there appears an embrace with Maggie Cheung. Still other images return, at times obsessively; of those loved and then lost in *Ashes of Time*, where an allegedly magic wine is supposed to have the power to efface them. But the images are persistent, they become resistant, secrete antibodies and do not allow themselves to be forgotten. They glide above the whole film, and return at regular intervals to fissure the characters' present. Stranger still is the sequence at the end of *Days of Being Wild*. As the jungle passes by the window, Yudi, just before dying, has a vision. He sees the image of what had always been hidden from him: his real mother abandoning him into the arms of the mother who brought him up in exchange for money. As he dies, his secret is suddenly revealed to us. This flash-back is once again shown outside any enunciative context, like a divine revelation, an ultra-lucid flash from who knows where. One of Wong Kar-wai's major aims is to organize large webs around which images move, scattering their seeds and growing amongst the ordered sequences like a wild and uncontrollable vegetation. Legend has it that at the moment of death, the brain re-runs all the images of life in a single second. Wong Kar-wai's shots give that same impression: a concerted disturbance of the senses driven by an incredible release of energy.

This fantasy of pure image, *shown before having been seen*, as if directly gathered from the remotest regions of the brain, is not unrelated to the way new images are in fact produced. Because they are no longer the product of recorded reality, digital images have never been seen either, appearing on the surface of the visible without ever having transited through the gaze. This congruency between the film-maker's style and the most contemporary forms of communication brings an entirely original relationship to bear on what has forever made up the texture of movies: time and space. They have been blown to pieces. Space is purely abstract, almost virtual, systematically curved by the effect of short focal distances. There is no more inside and outside, like in the first shots of *Fallen Angels* where the subway train actually seems to cross the room Michelle Li is walking around as the camera moves incessantly from interior to exterior. Places are always poorly marked off (for instance building's common areas in *Happy Together*, the way the same film makes no distinction between the kitchen of the restaurant where Fai works and the one in her apartment which she shares with her neighbors), and are in any case easily accessible (Yudi's apartment in *Days of Being Wild* which his neighbor enters through the window as if it were the most normal thing in the world). And the whole world itself appears like the everywhere identical global village described by Virilio. Hong-Kong is in Buenos Aires and vice versa. One is at best the flip-side of the other (nice sequence where Fai imagines Hong-Kong walking upside down). Nothing allows us to distinguish these different urban spaces, and all signs of Argentinean-ness in *Happy Together* are reduced to a handful of postcard images.

Time fares no better in this aesthetic big bang. Wong Kar-wai has broken off definitively — and it is a true epistemological rupture — with the idea (put forth by Bazin and reworked by Daney) that a film shot is not an image but rather a block of homogeneous time. Developing a very personal use of slow-motion in the laboratory, Wong Kar-wai has the various components of his shots running at different speeds. In *Chungking Express* for instance, Tony Leung drinks his coffee in slow motion in the foreground, while behind him, passers-by move in accelerated motion. The shot thereby ceases to be a receptacle able to record one and the same length of time; it becomes instead an instrument for fabricating antagonistic lengths of time. Time in Wong Kar-wai's last films has nothing much to do with that of Newtonian

physics, linear and uniform, like the line of a graph going unbroken from the past into the future. Its structure is much fuzzier; it draws time zones, zones of turbulence, common to all accidents. One slides more than one moves forward in it, the split between the past and the future is not the consequence of a cut, and the process of transformation from one to the other could only be described as fluctuating. One could speak of a true depth of time in Wong Kar-wai's films, and *Happy Together* is a film told at several speeds. The narrative stops and starts; the characters are unable to leave one another. Like tango dancers, they step forward then backward, never moving forward. And in spite of everything, time slips inexorably away between their fingers; but we don't see it passing like the cars in Buenos Aires, filmed in sped-up motion and transformed into mere beams of multicolor light.

A World of Individuals. What stands up against this flood of image and sound are the characters. They are the cornerstone of every film. And all the formal commotion Wong Kar-wai puts together only serves to emphasize their destitution and their emotional impoverishment. Few film-makers have been able to define, as he has, the sentiment of modern man and his status as an individual. The individual is a lone man, without family or community, the man of modern societies as described by contemporary sociology (Gilles Lipovetski, *Era of the Individual*). Wong Kar-wai's planet is peopled only by singles and orphans. The characters belong to only one generation, from twenty to thirty years old, and the preceding generation, that of their parents, seems to have disappeared. When a few members still remain, their only function is to make the youngest ones suffer more. In *Days of Being Wild*, the biological mother abandoned her son and refused to see him while the adoptive mother is an unworthy old alcoholic, surrounded by young hustlers. As for the fathers, they remain obstinately absent (the father in *Happy Together* never accepted his son's life) or are condemned to be absent (the father in *Fallen Angels* dies and becomes a mere video image his son plays in a loop). Finally in *Ashes of Time*, being an orphan leads to the brink of madness: the eldest daughter of the Murong clan (Brigitte Li), the only survivor of her decimated family, splits in two incarnating an imaginary brother. It is not surprising that this rootless generation finds it hard to build relationships. For all the crossing paths in Wong Kar-wai's films, lasting meetings are rare. Loves are always foiled. The numerous ephemeral couples in *Days of Being Wild* fall apart.

The heroes of *Ashes of Time* live in a constant rehashing of burnt out loves. Leslie Cheung sums it up at the end of the film, by saying, *"it is my fate to be single"*. The Wongian hero is condemned to celibacy. Though *Happy Together* related the chronic of a couple, the film's time-frame is that of the couple falling apart. After breaking off with Po-Wing, Fai's encounter with a young cook turns sour and at the end everyone is single once again. If there is indeed a utopia Wong Kar-wai's characters will never get to, it is *happy together*. They are systematically *unhappy alone*.

This fundamental solitude and existential void in which the modern individual makes his way, is given an eloquent form through the use of a cinematic device little used in Hong-Kong before Wong Kar-wai: the voice-off. In virtually every film, all the main characters are assigned a voice-off. They comment on what they're doing, provide information not given by the narrative, anticipate their own existence, share their regrets… This polyphony of interior voices often has striking poetic force. But it also comments on the characters' terrible loneliness. When interior monologue takes the place of dialogue, it is because communication is no longer self-evident. The voices-off seal the characters in on themselves. They also detach them from experiencing the present. *"In 48 hours, I was going to fall in love with this woman"*; *"May 15th 1995, I almost fell in love for the first time"*; *"I would never forget that minute next to her"*; *"In a year will you still remember this moment next to me?"* Phrases intended for no one but the speaker, making it clear that the characters are outside what they are living, spectators of their own existence. In such a refusal to allow complete involvement in what is being lived through lies the film-maker's most profoundly nostalgic outlook. Because true nostalgia, the *saudade*, is not a nostalgia for the past (which is a fairly sterile feeling) but rather the nostalgia for the present, the melancholic awareness that the present is always what is in the process of coming apart, of ceasing to exist.

This disjunction of the individual from the present and from his own experience is also revealed in systematically discordant gestures. *In Chungking Express*, *Fallen Angels* and *Happy Together*, the characters move incessantly. They run in every direction and yet never manage to do anything. The lovers in *Happy Together* tear each other apart but don't split up. The hysterical young girl in *Fallen Angels* (Charlie Young) flails around but all her efforts go contrary to her wishes. Finally, the problem for the characters in *Chungking Express*, is that they are always in motion and never in action. Cop 223 (Takeshi Kaneshiro) makes call after call to his girlfriends and never manages to reach a single one who is willing to meet him. He buys over two dozen tins of pineapple to send to the girl he loves, who has left him, but ends up eating them all by himself in one sitting. Later he takes a woman (Brigitte Lin) up to a hotel room but spends the night watching her sleep while stuffing himself on Chef's Salads. The young waitress (Faye Wang) spends her days messing up the apartment of #663 (Tony Leung) only to put everything back in place in the evening. #663 abruptly leaves his station to check and see if his former girlfriend has not returned to their apartment, although he knows perfectly well this is impossible. All the characters operate on a principle of pure expenditure: they rush helter-skelter, but their uncoordinated movements get them nowhere. As if gestures could no longer be extended into actions and only ever led to irrational acts; as if the characters suffered from some motor malfunctioning which dragged them into a spiral of confusion and restlessness. One lone character seems to be on the side of control: the fascinating woman criminal concealed under a blond wig and behind dark glasses. The speed with which she kidnaps a child, and the authority with which she oversees readying a drug cache is utterly staggering. But when she gets to the airport to ship off the heroin, the smugglers have vanished. In the end, her professional skill and diligence are for naught. She was no more able to control the thread of precipitous gestures she had brought into play than the other characters could. The movements now have value only in and of themselves; they are unable to have any impact on reality; at best they compose a mechanical ballet in which every gesture becomes abstract, losing its purpose in favor of a purely musical significance.

That's how it is in Wong Kar-wai's films. The images break loose from any context of enunciation to drift through the narrative; space splits into pieces; the film's direction is no longer governed by a spatial scenography based on continuity, but becomes an abstract device of pure optic and sonic sensations; as in the sublime verse from *Hamlet*, *"the time is out of joint"* and it breaks up into atoms of disparate and overlapping lengths

of time. And yet, the land from which Wong Kar-wai speaks to us remains that of cinema, not that of the visual. Whatever his detractors may claim, he is not merely a fancy advertiser, or a grand image-maker. He films the huge flow of contemporary images from the inside, hones them to an almost dizzying point of seductiveness, but at the same time is not afraid to talk about the damage they do. Individuals are alone, orphaned, unfit for love, unable to exert the slightest influence on reality (always somewhere else out of reach). In these film prisms which collect the luminous reflections of cityscapes and the somber psyches of his characters, diffracting them in the brightly colored facets of a video clip, there remains what is the true measure of any great film-maker: a perfectly articulated vision of the state of the world, here and today.

CHASING THE METAPHYSICAL EXPRESS: MUSIC IN THE FILMS OF WONG KAR-WAI

*W*ong Kar-wai has invented a notion hitherto completely unknown in the Hong-Kong film industry: that of *auteur*. For many years already, other film-makers had been adapting standard genres and forms to fit their personal vision, but always within production structures and a marketing system which never considered cinema as anything more than an 'entertainment product'. But none had deliberately set out to create an *œuvre*. Hong-Kong films in those days were always shot very quickly, by one or more directors and assistants, from constantly recycled screenplays, using interchangeable actors and the bare minimum of scenery. In this rush for commercial viability the great loser was always the post-production process (cutting, sound effects, background music), generally perfunctory and largely unsupervised by the director. For many years copyright laws were totally ignored. It was therefore not uncommon to find famous Chinese or western film music, or even hit songs, dubbed onto half a dozen different films the same year. The same was true of traditional music and classical Chinese opera. This carried on until the end of the 1980s, despite the fact that the industry had already been dominated for a decade by a 'New Wave' of film-makers trained outside the studio system, either abroad or in television. Even the most 'personal' of directors were forced to bow to the demands of the market-place and put commercial viability before any artistic pretensions they may have had.

Wong Kar-wai, for his part, started out in films as a script-writer, a highly unusual activity in Hong-Kong where films are often shot directly from a synopsis, with the bones of plot and dialogue being written from one day to the next in the course of shooting. Since 1988 when he made the first feature-length film, *As Tears Go By*, he has scripted all his films, and controlled all other aspects of their production on the *auteur* model. He explores a universe of personal themes and obsessions, selects the actors, locations and duration of the shoot (often changed to allow for improvisation), takes sole charge of the final cut and, of course, the background music and songs, selecting the composer (generally either Danny Chung or Frankie Chan) and the songs or extracts that he wants to use. This unique position as an enlightened artist has enabled him, in the course of just six films, to achieve total creative freedom, making him a cult director able to manipulate the system by playing around with its codes, inventing new roles and imposing his own marketing criteria. Very much along the lines of the French Nouvelle Vague, which brought to 1960s cinema the iconoclastic arrogance and rebellious glamour of a burgeoning pop culture.

Above all, Wong Kar-wai has opened up a new emotional dimension in Hong-Kong cinema, which previously functioned entirely according to the codes of classical drama. His use of music is characteristic of this approach, which aims the whole time to bring out an unstated emotion. Unlike other Hong-Kong directors, Wong Kar-wai never uses Chinese music, because in his films the sound-track never illustrates a precise, real context, but evokes a purely referential, even interior world. In *Days of Being Wild* (1990), the 'original music' is actually a compilation of cha-cha and rumba tunes by the great orchestrator Xavier Cugat. The film is set in 1960 but the music, from the 40s and 50s, conjures up an atmosphere with no direct link to the real context. The mixture of the two is what generates a coherent world, a fantasy re-creation of the 60s which owes more to the glamour of Italian cinema or the musicals of the period than any kind of historical truth. The same goes for *Happy Together* (1997), his latest film, set in Argentina. If on this occasion he makes abundant use of the famous tangos of Astor Piazzola to anchor his story in a typically Argentinean environment, it is ultimately a symbolic rather than a realistic gesture. The country is simplified until it is just the birthplace of tango, with music dominating all other aspects and justifying on its own the shift in the director's universe (all Wong Kar-wai's other films take place in either Hong-Kong or China). This makes Wong stand out as a true creator of cinematic artefacts, stylised visions of the world which derive their internal coherence from the atmosphere created by the music.

In *Ashes of Time* (1994) he decided to bring this technique to bear on the sword-fighting film, a key genre in local cinema. For what was his third feature, he commissioned composer Frankie Chan, a former martial arts choreographer, to write a score inspired by Ennio Morricone's spaghetti western music, rather than the Chinese music traditionally used to provide 'local colour'. In his work, the destructuring and modernisation of genres involves re-interpreting codes, a process in which music is central. But this re-reading is not just a matter of musical disorientation. It also involves setting up historical shortcuts (such as the allusion to the western) which allow the director to convey his intentions simply by quoting a piece of music. In Wong Kar-wai's films the sound-track is therefore not just used for purposes of illustration, it establishes a constant dialogue (a *mise en abime*) with both the audience and the characters. In *Chungking Express* (1994), 'California Dreaming' by The Mamas and the Papas, which comes back and back like a litany, both generates and reveals the urge for escape felt by the young waitress, played by Faye Wong. She literally *dreams* of *California*, and even ends up going there, *because of* the song. This kind of resonance is sometimes given an ironic twist, providing an external counterpoint to the story. That happens with the Turtles' classic 'Happy Together', which brings to a close the failed love story of *Happy Together*. Here, film and song have the same title, showing, if further evidence were needed, the key importance of choice of music for Wong. A man of wide-ranging musical knowledge, he tends to work in the same way each time. He will choose a record, select several extracts, then 'place' them in the film according to a precise rationale which turns pre-existing pieces into 'musical themes'. He did this in *Days of Being Wild*, where the sound-track comes entirely (except for one piece by Django Reinhardt) from a compilation album by Xavier Cugat. The same 'method' was used in *Happy Together*, most of whose tangos are taken from one record: *Tango Apasionado* by Astor Piazzola.

Of course, the interaction between music and the characters is expressed visually just as much as symbolically. In Wong Kar-wai's films the characters create their own sound environment. They hear and above all listen to music. Music exacerbates their narcissistic impulses, brings out their natural sensuality and consolidates the fantasy worlds that they invent for themselves. Music creates pockets of fiction within the overall fiction of the story, mini-narratives for the characters. One scene in particular from *Days of Being Wild* illustrates the key role it plays in the psychological constitution of Wong's heroes. Yuddy (Leslie Cheung), a romantic and rebellious playboy alone in his room after one of his girlfriends has left, turns on an old record-player with a record already on. There emerges a tune by Xavier Cugat, to which he begins languidly dancing while watching himself in the mirror. This type of scene, in which one or more characters listen to music in a world of their own, temporarily detached from reality, recurs on a regular basis, from *Chungking Express* (Faye Wong dancing while making her sandwiches or doing the cleaning) to *Happy Together* (the lovers united in a melancholy tango), making Wong Kar-wai's films constantly flirt with the musical genre without ever slipping into it completely.[1]

[1] Wong Kar-wai's next feature film, *Summer in Beijing*, will finally be a musical, as if his first six films had gradually been working in that direction all along.

Moreover, as in Gene Kelly musicals, the music in Wong Kar-wai's films always makes a break in the scene, interrupting the story-line. This is where they differ most markedly from video clip techniques, with which however they otherwise have much in common. Each film contains one or more 'sung' passages, from *As Tears go by*, with the Cantonese version of 'Take My Breath Away' (a song by the group Berlin from the film *Top Gun*), to *Happy Together* with its hit by The Turtles, to Faye Wong's songs (by The Cranberries and Cocteau Twins) in *Chungking Express*, or again Frankie Chan's re-orchestration of 'Karma Koma' (by Massive Attack) for *Fallen Angels*. The justification for these sequences is partly commercial in that the audience loves Canto-Pop, the local pop variety, but it also goes back to the Hong-Kong cinema tradition which is full of scenes of this type. Wong Kar-wai has simply taken the system to extremes, turning each of his films into a cinematic *and* musical experience at the same time. This is shown by the fact that *Chungking Express* has recently been copied shot by shot for a video by the group Texas: a pointless piece of plagiarism which, however, demonstrates the inherent musicality of Wong's films.

Another similarity with video-clips is that Wong Kar-wai's characters adopt one of two positions: either that of the star (they have to do a 'number', take centre stage – e.g. the killer (man or woman), the swordsman, the salesgirl behind her counter), or that of the audience. Every gesture and every expression is carefully thought out by the actors like a movement on stage, not in the theatre but at a rock concert. In *Days of Being Wild* the young dancer Mimi (Carina Lau) introduces herself to the young man who will later fall head over heels in love with her by doing an improvised dance number. In *Fallen Angels* (1995) the hired killer (Leon Lai) waits in a corridor (the wings) before entering a hairdressing salon (the stage) and killing everyone, only to vanish afterwards. Thus the characters live by and for the music. They move to its rhythm and when it stops, they slip away. That is why the actors are often pop stars, equally famous for their musical careers as for their screen appearances. This applies to Andy Lau (*As Tears Go By*, *Days of Being Wild*), Jackie Cheung (*As Tears Go By*, *Days of Being Wild*, *Ashes of Time*), Leslie Cheung (*Days of Being Wild*, *Ashes of Time*, *Happy Together*), Leon Lai (*Fallen Angels*) and above all Faye Wong, whose appearance in *Chungking Express* remains her only film experience to date.

The same thing happens to the directing as to the actors: both are *in tune* with the sound-track, perfectly synchronised with its changes of tempo. Time is always crucial in Wong Kar-wai's films and music is used almost as a unit of measurement. It may emerge from a radio, a CD player, a juke-box (in *As Tears Go By* and *Chungking Express* these are presented as true pagan altars), or even from nowhere in particular, but it never arrives 'out of the blue': it builds up gradually. There are no scenes which both begin and end with music. The only really musical moments in his cinema are the 'interludes' between one chapter in the story and the next, located at key points in the film and designed to give rhythm to the narrative, or rather to stop it from running away, out of control. They include the long travelling-shots of the Thai forest to the sound of guitar music in *Days of Being Wild*, the speeded-up desert shots in *Ashes of Time*, and the waterfalls in *Happy Together*, all of which plunge the audience into a state of passive contemplation, allowing the director to open up a second, purely sensory level of reading. In *Chungking Express* there are moments of 'disconnection' like this where the heroes move in slow motion while the city pulsates at an accelerated rate. This special effect (which involves filming an actor moving extremely slowly at normal speed, then running the film speeded-up) allows the director to place his heroes inside a 'bubble', an inner world where music expresses feelings. The camera caresses the actors (see Michelle Lee's very beautiful masturbation scene in *Fallen Angels*), enveloping them so that they become 'prisoners of the rhythm'. The director can then decide to stop them in mid-action with freeze-frame images, break down their movements with strobe effects or inserts, or even flood them with light and leave them to face the audience alone.

21 ▶▶

This intrinsic complementarity between sound-world and story is probably what makes it possible to watch Wong Kar-wai's films many times over without becoming bored. Each one works like a piece of music, with a refrain, repeats, and a catchy tune. They establish Wong Kar-wai as the inventor of a new form of cinema, the musical chronicle, which differs from the musical itself principally in that the actors do not sing (at least, not on stage). He certainly makes use of other features of the genre. His dialogues in particular, made up of aphorisms and poetic phrases, often resemble song couplets, possessing the same lightness of touch, the same *profound* superficiality. For it is clear that the music of the words counts for more than their meaning. One of the characters in *Happy Together* puts it very nicely: 'You can see much better with your ears...'. Music speaks just as evocatively as pictures, and in fact always has the *last* word. All Wong Kar-wai's films have one thing in common: they all end on a song which, from *Days of Being Wild* onwards, has always opened up the perspective of a fresh departure, a new story just beginning, for once giving the lie to the fateful title 'The End'. For music alone is capable of transcending the limits of fiction.

THE EROTICS OF DISAPPOINTMENT

Wong Kar Wai's cinematographer Christopher Doyle has come up with a working image to describe Wong's films: The structure of a Wong Kar Wai film is like a fat man's feet. They more or less get him from place to place but he can't see them till the end of the day. Now that Wong has finished six feature films (with a seventh currently being made) it may be time to ask where the fat man's feet have taken him.

One plausible, but in the end, unsatisfactory way of thinking about the series is to see each subsequent film as a new departure, a refusal to repeat what went before. Thus, the first gangster or hero film *As Tears Go By* (1988) was followed by the second nostalgia film *Days of Being Wild* (1991), set in the Hong Kong of the 1960's which, in terms of subject matter, narrative techniques, and the pace and rhythm of the editing could not be more different. The third film *Ashes of Time* (1994), which explored and exploded the martial arts genre, was different again. And so it goes, through to *Chungking Express* (1994), which has become a kind of Hong Kong cult movie.

Fallen Angels (1996), and the latest release, *Happy Together* (1997), Wong's version of the gay road movie, set of all places in Buenos Aires. Each film it seems would take a genre, and then take it elsewhere. Looked at in this way, the film series will fit the conventional idea of what constitutes originality: constant innovation, an emphasis on change and development. One wonders though how long such innovation can go on before it exhausts itself.

There is, however, another radically different way of thinking about the series, which is to see it as essentially not concerned with change and development at all. From this point of view each film in the series is an attempt to describe a spatial and affective order of things which stubbornly refuses definition and resolution. At the same time, the more elusive the order of things, the more intense the fascination. Every film then is a fragment, incomplete in itself; a return to a site whose features have been glimpsed before, but only partially. The structural principles of the series are not change and development, but rather repetition and memory, which nevertheless hold their own different kind of surprise — witness the many shifts of attention, the modifications of narrative procedures, the experiments with the expressive/repressive possibilities of the film image; in short, the seemingly endless defile of unpredictable traits or symptoms that parade across a Wong Kar Wai film. These structural principles also affect the way we read Wong's work. Repetition means that each subsequent film refines and redefines the way we look at earlier ones. We might then, from the vantage point of *Happy Together* and Hong Kong in 1997 re-view a series that began with *As Tears Go By* in 1988 — almost another era.

Before we can do that, however, it will be necessary to consider a set of questions first. To begin with, how is such a seemingly arty cinema possible in a Hong Kong notorious for its commercialism, where the laws of the market place necessarily extend to film production? This allows us to bring into the discussion an absolutely essential factor for understanding the new Hong Kong cinema, namely, the period between 1984-1997: between the Sino-British declaration of 1984, announcing the return of Hong Kong to Chinese sovereignty, and its actual reversion to Chinese rule from July 1997 onwards, with the catastrophe of Tiananmen Square occurring midway in 1989. During this period, while it remained true that the Hong Kong cinema had to be commercial and popular if it was to exist at all, there was also a new element: it was a cinema that addressed a public in the process of changing; a public suddenly anxious about its cultural identity, because so many future social and political issues seemed to hinge on the question of identity. The result, then, was that serious themes and complex cinematic styles could now be entertained and entertaining as some sectors at least of the cinema-going public became more open to the representation of problematic and contradictory situations. Thus, together with a lot of forgettable and run-of-the-mill productions, a number of innovative films with various degrees of commercial and artistic success began to appear which took for their theme the personal, cultural and political dilemmas of Hong Kong; films like Stanley Kwan's *Rouge* (1988), Evans Chan's *To Liv (e)* (1990), Ann Hui's *Song of the Exile* (1990) and Tsui Hark's seemingly interminable martial arts series, *Once Upon a Time in China* (1991).

However, even if we set Wong Kar Wai's films against this very creative moment of Hong Kong cinema, certain characteristics still stand out. The first is that we find no direct reference in any of these films to the political situation at all. This is quite remarkable, given the fact that even a highly stylized film like *Rouge* manages to smuggle in an allusion to 1997 — in the figure of the ghost who returns physically unchanged fifty years after her suicide, to search for her lover, an obvious reference to the fifty years without change promised to Hong Kong by Deng Xiao Ping; and even a campy Sci-Fi fantasy, like Tsui Hark's *Wicked City* (1992), which rips off everything from *Casablanca* and *King Kong* to *Bladerunner*, has to insert the 1997 political changeover as part of its plot. By contrast, politics seems to be conspicuously absent in Wong's films. What we do find, on the other hand, is something else, a more indirect relation to the political. More than any other Hong Kong director, Wong conveys in his films a particularly intense experience of the period as an experience of the negative; an experience of some elusive and ambivalent cultural space that lies always just beyond our grasp, or just beneath our articulations. It is this lived experience of the negative, in its many manifestations in public and private life, that is the enduring subject of Wong's cinema, the subject that obsessively returns.

The negative, as I am suggesting, has some relation to the politics of the period. Looking back now, and in the light of information which was not available earlier, we can see that some of the confusions of the time were structural. We now know that China and Britain (represented at that point by Sir Geoffery Howe) entered into secret negotiations over Hong Kong, and reached some kind of tacit agreement that, among other things, the pace of democratization in Hong Kong would not be

speeded up. Unfortunately, nobody seemed to have informed Chris Patten, the last colonial governor of Hong Kong, about this, and he proceeded to lead the Empire's last hurrah by promptly introducing electoral reforms. The result then was a legacy of confusion and recrimination, with each side accusing the other of bad faith. Something of these confusions, a part of what I am calling the experience of the negative, has seeped into Wong's films. The rapid, but also uneven, transformations of Hong Kong's cultural space, as a result of the push — and — pull politics, show themselves in these films symptomatically as spatial paradoxes and contradictions, or as the skewing of affective relations. Thus, one of Wong's most constant themes, found in all his films in different modalities, is proximity without reciprocity; that is to say, how we can be physically close to a situation or to a person without there being any intimacy or knowledge. "At our most intimate," one character says of another, in *Chungking Express*, whom he first encounters as an anonymous body in a quick moving crowd, "we were only 0.01 cm apart."

Complementing and exacerbating this experience of the negative is the experience of speed. By speed here, I am referring not to the quick-cutting style or the propensity for violent action that so many critics associate with the Hong Kong cinema. What I have in mind are the transformations of cultural space that result from the new technologies: not only the technologies that increase the speed of movement, but also the technologies that increase the speed of reproduction and information. In Wong's cinema, speed (like politics) is also represented obliquely, in terms of the characters barely conscious social adjustments or maladjustments to the new speed-dominated cultural space, a space that seems to have lost its measure. Space now becomes incommensurable, unprecedented, exorbitant. For example, we see characters (especially in the later films) stricken by a kind of pathological or genetic reticence, as if the language of affect had been forgotten or had never been properly acquired in the first place. We think of Ah Faye in *Chungking Express* coyly communicating with others and with herself through the medium of cover-version songs (*California Dreaming, Dream Lover*); Ouyang Feng, the martial arts hero in *Ashes of Time*, wrapped up in ressentiment because he is afraid of speaking words of love; and the dumb boy in *Fallen Angels*, videotaping his father at the most awkward moments. There is also the heroine of *As Tears Go By*, who first appears wearing a medical gauze mask covering her mouth, like some survivor of a nuclear holocaust. Dialogue between characters on screen gives way to a kind of metalingual off-screen voice-over, as if everyday language were a kind of gibberish that required glossing and commentary. The damaged dialogue and the often misleading and misguided commentaries show, on the verbal level, one of the paradoxes of speed: its relation (as Virilio has noted) to inertia. This relation between speed and (affective) inertia is a constant in Wong's cinema.

Speed too is registered in Wong's filmic images, as their silent accompaniment. Something, decidedly, has happened to them, and this brings us to the third point. If we say that Wong's images are a response to a space transformed by speed and historical confusion, this is emphatically not merely to take note of the occasional use he makes of quick cutting or step-printing techniques. Speed in the sense we are trying to define it is not synonymous with movement; it has more to do with the subtle instabilities of the image, which challenge cognition and recognition, whatever its state of motion. Take, for example, the first shot of Wong's first film, which juxtaposes a neon-lit Mainland Chinese department store sign on the left, with multiple television screens that flicker without content on the right. This is an ordinary enough image of urban Hong Kong, except that it just so happens that in the same instant, it moves through two historical grids, superimposing the slower, older world of material objects found in emporiums, and the dematerialized, placeless and instantly commutable space of the televisual onto each other. It is not a question of rapid change and metamorphosis — a commonplace theme — but rather of anamorphosis, of how the historical grids by which we understand the image have themselves undergone change without our noticing. We find visual polyvalence, to be sure, but of a specific kind, where the multiple meanings do not cohere or support each other. We never find synesthesia, but always disjunction, dissemination, fugue. This results in a characteristic effect: in Wong's cinema, we are never certain about what we are seeing. The image always subtly misses its mark. It misses its appointment with meaning, and turns into that characteristic Wong Kar Wai thing, the image of disappointment. What is remarkable, however, is the constant inventiveness with which Wong pursues these images of disappointment, which impress us in the end with a kind of salutary incoherence.

All that we have said — the negative, speed, the filmic image — have their implications for narrative. With the exception of *As Tears Go By*, all Wong's films have a kind of loose, improvisatory narrative structure to them, as if they had lost their way (cf. the fat man's feet). One famous example is the final sequence of *Days of Being Wild*, where at the end of the story a new character is inexplicably introduced. Is this the lead-in to a sequel which has not yet been made? Or is it merely a non-sequitur? Or perhaps it is the irruption of some other story, a submerged fragment that has to come up at some point to the surface for air? In any case, the narrative does not contain the subject; the narrative leaks, and the subject appears and disappears in these leaks. This is not to say however that Wong's films are badly or loosely made; they are certainly more carefully and thoughtfully made than almost any other example of Hong Kong cinema. Rather, what we are reminded of is Walter Benjamin's insight into story-telling: that a crisis in story-telling is a crisis in experience, a crisis in our ability to communicate experience. Benjamin went on to study, particularly in the texts of Proust and Kafka, how the demise of traditional story-telling, as a consequence of changing social and cultural conditions, necessitated the invention of new and seemingly aberrant forms of story-telling. He described Kafkas stories as fairy-tales for dialecticians. Wong's cinema too, in the Hong Kong of the late eighties and the nineties, presents us with its own crisis of story-telling and experience. The readily intelligible stories now come from the standard genres, which is mostly Wong's starting point — the gangster story, the love story, the martial arts story and so on. But these stories are criss-crossed and cut up by other more fugitive tales, like so many loose threads. These tales are typically about ordinary lives that have gone slightly askew. *Chungking Express* and *Fallen Angels*, particularly, are populated with such characters, who live on the verge of hysteria. These characters are themselves constantly telling stories; and if they cannot find listeners, they become their own captive audience. This is ultimately why we find all those voice-overs that try to tell us things, or try to shape the world into some semblance of desire. But if images, or showing, have lost their authority, so too has telling. In Wong's cinema, the voice-over comes not from outside the story, commenting objectively and authoritatively on it, but from within the story, and subject to its aleatory flows.

Out of this crisis of narrative, with all that it implies, comes two of the most fascinating effects of Wong's cinema. The first is a certain kind of boredom, very marked from Wong's second film onwards. It is not the boredom of nothing happening, but the nervous boredom of not knowing what is happening, of losing the thread. Time weighs heavy not because it is empty, but because it has gone through strange loops. Eventualities now precede the event, outpacing it, anticipating it. When the event eventually occurs, the result is always anticlimactic, disappointing, boring. June 30 1997 in Hong Kong is the privileged example here, perhaps a matrix for all those instances of disappointment in Wong's films, like the visit to the Iguazu Waterfalls in *Happy Together*. A second related effect is melancholia that all Wong's major characters display to a greater or lesser degree, and it bears on the experience of space (as boredom bears on the experience of time). To recall Freud, if mourning is grief over a lost object (like a loved one), melancholia is a sense of loss without an object; hence, a grief with no name; hardly assuagable by eating thirty cans of pineapples, like the jilted policeman in the first part of *Chungking Express*; or by turning from hero to venal death-broker, like Ouyang Feng in *Ashes of Time*.

A final point concerns the city, perhaps the most important of Wong's melancholic objects. With the exception of *Ashes of Time*, every film is set in the city, in a Hong Kong that is at once both recognizable and unfamiliar. It may be a Hong Kong distanced in time, as in *Days of Being Wild*, which takes place in the sixties. Or it may be an antipodal image of Hong Kong, like the Buenos Aires of *Happy Together*, literally on the other side of the earth. But the city remains in all cases the space of desire. It can even be argued that, in spite of its backdrop of mountains and deserts, the kind of perverse affective relations that develop in *Ashes of Time* can only be associated with the space of the city. The city then is not only a physical space, but also a psychic one. This is one reason why the city is never shown whole, but only in fragments, in metonymies and displacements. In Wong's films, there is not a single shot of the Hong Kong skyline, that picture postcard metaphor of Hong Kong, conjuring up images of power and desire. Wong's Hong Kong is a city of a different kind, and the secret of that city is not power, but impotence.

These five points — the experience of the negative and of speed, the problematic nature of the image and narrative, the city as space of desire — are, it seems to me, the main elements of a combinatoire that every Wong Kar-wai film so far returns obsessively to. It is time to look at the individual films in greater detail.

Watching *As Tears Go By* now, it is surprising how well it still holds up, even though in terms of narrative, it is the most conventional of all Wong's films. The genre that Wong is working in is the hero film popularized by John Woo in his *A Better Tomorrow* series, the first of which appeared in 1986. Woo's series is not just a celebration of violence, in spite of its reputation in the West. Glimpsed through the violence is a sense of the break-up of society and the social morality that prevailed in the Hong Kong of the late eighties. Social morality became, to some extent, a matter of: who knows? who cares? This has two consequences in Woos films that save them from cynicism. The first is a kind of amoralism that allows Woo

to film the shoot-outs and killings with an exhilarating absence of moral inhibitions, as pure spectacle; hence those famous aestheticisations of action and choreography of movements all shot in slow motion. The second consequence, on the social level, is a retreat to a kind of neo-tribalism, with the emphasis being placed, not on loyalty to a larger community, but on local and personal loyalties — to the gang, to a brother, to a friend; i.e., to all the members of what Karl Taro Grenfield calls a speed tribe. There is always a clear-cut plot in a John Woo film revolving around a central conflict between loyalty and betrayal; there are good bad guys and bad bad guys. But in spite of this antinomianism, we do not find in the end a critique of moral values coming as a response to new social conditions, but rather a return to a less complex moral system that largely precludes the need to register any kind of ambiguity. As The Killer, a later film in the series about a professional killer protecting a blind girl, shows, John Woos films are essentially conservative and sentimental — which is one reason for their successful transplantation to Hollywood.

As Tears Go By, in spite of its story about two hoods trying to make it in the mean streets of Hong Kong's Mongkok, cannot be mistaken for a John Woo movie. The first thing we notice is a visual density that produces an overall sense of spatial ambiguity and discontinuities, like the juxtaposed images of the neon-lit Chinese emporium sign and multiple television screens already alluded to, or the surprising image of the heroine who first appears wearing an unromantic medical gauze mask. This ambiguity is continued in the films use of color, which looks by turns under — and over- exposed, either too red or too blue, never just right. Affectively, the hero is pulled in different directions between lover and friend. He moves back and forth in a disconcerting cadence between idyllic Lantau Island where the lover lives, and the triad-controlled streets of Mongkok where the friend is always getting into trouble with the mob. It is not a simple question now of loyalty. The two spaces define the terms of an aporia, because loyalty to one is inevitably betrayal of the other. The only choice that can be made is who to betray. Moreover, after a point the two spaces cannot be held separate. In the film, both love and violence erupt suddenly, and they are shot in the same way, in slow motion, which nevertheless fails to capture what is essential about either. It is as if both action and affection have now become so problematic that slowing them down reveals nothing further, no insight into how things work. It is these irresolutions, understood in both a visual and cognitive sense, that characterize the film. In this respect, the stylistic implications of *As Tears Go By*, with its images of irresolution, are the exact opposite of MTV to which it has often misleadingly been compared. MTV gives us a succession of images to hold our attention, which it realizes is limited. By contrast, in Wong's film even careful and unlimited attention to images cannot keep the world from surreptitiously, like the tears of the films title, going by.

In Wong's gangster film then, the moral ambiguity of classic film noir is reconstructed as a spatial and epistemological ambiguity. But the main point to emphasize is that in spite of the violent and often crude nature of the films action, *As Tears Go By* can be seen as Wong's first attempt to represent a negative space. From a larger political perspective, this negativity will have to be related to the problematic nature of a colonial space making the transition from imperialism to multinational capitalism, a space where all the rules have quietly changed. In the film itself, however, the political implications of negativity are expressed only indirectly, in the characters futile attempts to live their lives in the negativity of the city, which ultimately destroys them. Take the question of a persons power and position in the city's underworld (and perhaps not only in its underworld). Every big brother has his own little brother for whom he is a role model. But every little brother is also a big brother to his own little brother. Positions are precarious in a constantly shifting and uncertain hierarchy. Every gang member has to prove his mettle by performing ever more dangerous acts of bravado. The only source of certainty and power is death. Thus, one of the films most interesting episodes occurs toward the end, when, after a history of failure and humiliation, the hero's young friend decides to accept a suicide mission. With nothing left to lose, he returns to the mahjong parlor where a rival gang hangs out and publicly humiliates the gang leader who has been viciously harassing him. What protects, but also finally kills the young friend is of course the power of the negative, and at this point power and impotence shade into each other.

After the frantic action of the first film, *Days of Being Wild* came as something of a let down to Hong Kong audiences. Set in Hong Kong in the sixties, it struck many as being disappointingly slow. What it introduced, we can now see, are some of the hallmarks of Wong's later film style, particularly the use of an episodic, serial structure of repetition, with stories that half-connect to one another; the use of the voice-over as a narrative device; the use of paired shots and situations that do not match up, like the shots of Yuddy combing his hair at different moments, or Yuddy walking away with his back toward us. All these stylistic devices, together and separately, constitute what I believe is a new kind of image in the Hong Kong cinema, what we might call the disappointing image.

Take for example the great panning shot of dense green forests that accompanied the screening of the titles and credits near the beginning of the film. Just as we are beginning to think that it might be an image of unspoiled nature or pure origins, we see crossing the screen some lines that gradually become discernible as electric wires or telephone lines. The image deliberately raises expectations that are not met. This is paradigmatic of the films as a whole. Another good example is the meeting between Yuddy and Lai Jun that opens the film, immediately preceding the shot of green forests. It is one minute before 3 pm on 16 April 1960 that they first became friends and then lovers. The public minute that recurs every day is held on to as a special irrevocable moment in the lovers' private time, like a daily appointment with the origin of passion. But in the film all appointments are disappointments. Passion dies and private time is swallowed up once again, becoming indistinguishable from public time, no matter how willfully one or both lovers try not to forget. Disappointment is the perception that every origin that we want to believe is unique and individual is already a repetition, like an old song that returns. In fact, the structural use of popular music is one of the ways repetition is suggested in Wong's films. The scene between Yuddy and Lai Jun cuts abruptly into the shot of green forests, and in the background can be heard the old song *You are always in my heart*, set to a rhumba beat reminiscent of old dance — hall music. Repetition too is in the visual constructions: the scene which takes place in a well-known sports club, with its sixties-style Coca-cola coolers and advertisements, looks very much like a kind of Pop Art, for which repetition is an aesthetic principle. A third key example of disappointment is the story that Yuddy tells himself and others of the legless bird that has to keep flying or die. It is a story that romanticizes movement and justifies non-commitment; but it turns out in the end, after Yuddy's flight to the Philippines, that the legless bird is not an image of someone with boundless energy, but a creature that is still-born. Too much speed turns into inertia, and both action and affection end up in paralysis.

Instead of linear plots then, what we now find is a serial structure of repetition. Most of the film is taken up with permutating the sets of possible relations among the six main characters, in a series of affective tableaux. In every set of relation, however, the characters miss each other and fail to match up — as Yuddy's friend tells Mimi, after he had sold the car that Yuddy had given him, because he looked out of place in it; just as he is no match for Mimi herself. All affective binds are double-binds. As a result, no story has a happy conclusion and everybody comes off second best. Love then is either entirely selfish and exploitative (Yuddy and his foster mother); or it is a boringly predictable sequence of friendship, sex, cohabitation and marriage to be avoided at all costs (Yuddy and Lai Jun); or it is a struggle for domination, a competition about who cares less (Yuddy and Mimi); or it does not even arrive at the stage of being a relationship (Lai Jun and the policeman; Yuddy's friend and Mimi).

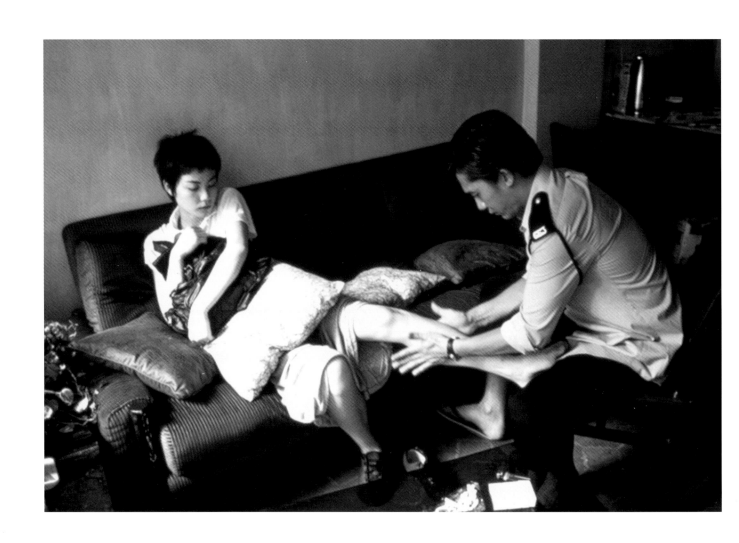

At the center of the series, it would seem, is Yuddy, who has an important and dominant relationship with each of the main characters. The first shot of Yuddy shows us his back. At critical moments, usually when a relationship is being broken, he combs his hair. Yuddy, it seems, is indifferent and narcissistic, a self-sufficient character in a world of the emotionally needy. "I dont know what he is thinking," Mimi tells Yuddy's friend, "but I know very well what you are thinking." Hence Yuddy's seductiveness. Yet it becomes quite clear that for all his studied indifference, Yuddy is the most needy and disappointing of all, an abandoned child raised by a foster mother, obsessed with knowing the identity of his biological mother. He does no work, and has been supported all his life by his foster mother. "What's the difference," she asks him after he has beaten up her gigolo, "between paying you and paying him? He gives me more pleasure." This pattern of dependency that looks like independence is repeated with Mimi. That is why he angrily throws her out of his apartment when she naively offers to support him by becoming a dance hall hostess. When the foster mother finally tells Yuddy the whereabouts of his real mother, he drops everything, including his relationship with Mimi, to look for her in the Philippines. She refuses to receive him, and we have another shot of Yuddy, very similar to the early shots, as he walks away from her estate, determined not to turn his head. The obvious pairing of these shots shows that self-possession is just the other face of a sense of loss. It is also at this point that we find another shot of the dense green forest that we had seen at the beginning of the film. The forest can now be placed specifically in the Philippines, and connotes a mother and an origin that Yuddy cannot find, something that the presence of the telephone lines in the first shot ironically prefigured. History for Yuddy turns hysterical. He gets drunk in Manila's Chinatown, loses his papers and all his money to a prostitute, and tries to cheat some Filipino thugs out of a fake passport without paying for it, an act of self-destruction. They catch up with him on the train leaving Manila and shoot him. The dominant center of the affective series turns out to be melancholic, obsessed with loss without an object.

 30

The film ends with a set of empty images: a train speeding through the green forest, Mimi in the Philippines futilely looking for Yuddy, Lai Jun at the sports club selling tickets and still dreaming, a public telephone that rings with no one to answer, and that final note of suspension: an unknown character out of nowhere introduced in the final minutes. We see him in a room with an extremely low ceiling. He puts on his jacket, puts money and a deck of cards in his waistcoat pockets, combs his hair and then switches off the light, while all the time, that repetitive and anachronistic music is heard in the background.

Ashes of Time re-examines many of the obsessions of *Days of Being Wild* through the martial arts genre. It introduces a radical note of negativity by making the traditionally extroverted, action-based kung fu film tell a convoluted story about the end of action and the weight of dead time. The Chinese title can roughly be rendered as Malevolent East, Malicious West. These are the fearsome sobriquets of the two main heroes Ouyang Feng and Huang Yaoshi, but they suggest as well the two points of a dystopic space. The film partly follows the martial arts narrative convention of recounting stories of legendary heroes, highlighting their martial arts skills. But there is a crucial change in the way heroism is represented. The more heroic the character, the more he seems damaged by life. The outstanding heroes (particularly the two heroes referred to in the film's Chinese title) are all, in one way or another, neurotics, living out their own private obsessions, which they project back onto the space around them.

The ambiguities of heroic space can be suggested by considering how action is represented. The early fight sequence, involving the film's main narrator Ouyang Feng, the Malicious West of the title, typifies the pattern. It is no longer a choreography of action that we see, as in other kung-fu or gangster movies, but a composition of light and color, into which all action has dissolved; a kind of Abstract Expressionism or Action Painting. Action has now become non-figurative. In all the fight scenes, it is only when the action slows down, that light resolves itself into something recognizably human; but when we do catch a glimpse of a human figure, it is always at the fatal moment of dealing out death, or in the throes of dying. As for the rest of the time, between the brief moments of blind action are the long moments of waiting for something to happen. In Ashes of Time, time is a heavy weight/wait, a void to be filled if only by a dead body. All the characters seem to be living their lives posthumously. Everybody waits, and it is not possible simply to associate the space of action with the male, and the time of waiting with the female, as is usually the case in the genre. Action itself has now been displaced. Affectivity is the other stage — bloodless but fatal — on which the action of the film unfolds.

The narrative is infected by the negative emotions of Ouyang Feng, who also dominates the voice-overs. The film opens with him engaged in a heroic fight; but after this first fight many years ago, the clean-shaven Ouyang Feng grows a mustache (the ash of time?) and we do not see him do any more fighting. Rather, he becomes a death broker, an entrepreneur dealing in killings and assassinations, concerned above all with spreading the spirit of malice. Everyone who has felt a twinge of envy or jealousy — and who hasn't? — understands the spirit of malice, Ouyang Feng says, addressing an invisible prospective client and, implicitly, the viewer, hypocrite voyeur, mon semblable, mon frere. He believes (wrongly it turns out) that his only friend, who comes to visit him once a year when the peach blossoms are in bloom, is Huang Yaoshi, because he thinks Huang is too proud to feel jealous. We learn only later why Ouyang Feng came to be the way he is. Ouyang Feng may have been a hero, but he was afraid of speaking words of love. This negligence wounds the woman he loves. She refuses to wait for him, and exacts her revenge by marrying his brother. This act, as precise as a practiced sword thrust, turns her life into a bitter triumph, and destroys his. Nothing, it seems, is more fearsome than feelings, and nothing is more destructive than a bad feeling.

This skewing of affectivity pervades the film, resulting in confusing displacements of desire, and this is reflected in the narrative which becomes extremely

convoluted. The film begins and ends with Ouyang Feng's speech as a death merchant, but all symmetries in the story turn out to be not flashes of meaning, but symmetries of misunderstanding and self-deception, obsessive repetitions. The schizoid figure of Murong Yang/Murong Yin is merely the most dramatic example. She is first introduced dressed in men's clothes, a standard martial arts story convention. In this guise, she meets the seductive Huang Yaoshi, who flirtatiously says to her, after a lot of wine together, that if she has a sister, he would certainly marry her. Murong Yang holds Huang to his promise and reappears as the lovely Murong Yin, but Huang does not show up at the appointed time. As Murong Yang again, she hires Ouyang Feng to arrange for Huang's assassination; but before Ouyang Feng agrees to accept the job, Murong Yin appears and offers to double his fee if he could have Murong Yang eliminated instead. Yang wants Huang killed to avenge her sister's disgrace; Yin wants Yang (her other self) killed to preserve the promise of happiness. Yin and Yang are deadlocked. As for Huang himself, the successful seducer, there is also no happiness. The seducer's principle, as he tells us in a voice-over, is that what cannot be obtained is always the most precious. His desire is for Ouyang Feng's sister-in-law, the woman dead to the world, hence he is secretly jealous of Ouyang whom the woman loves. His annual visits to Ouyang, out of friendship, is in fact an excuse to see her, to bring news of him to her. All sex, as Jacques Lacan tells us, involves at least four people, and desire is displaced in a series of metonymies. Huang loves peach blossoms, because the season when they bloom is when he visits her.

Ironically, it is only the ordinary figures who are relatively free of ressentiment, like the bare-foot mercenary Hong Qi, who makes his way in the world, unconventionally accompanied by his peasant wife. He too kills for money, but he can also agree to help a penniless young woman, who can only pay him with a basket of eggs, because he wants to. It is this ordinariness that escapes Ouyang Feng's influence, and that is the antithesis to heroism. Walter Benjamin, writing

about the ordinary heroism of modern life, said it took as much energy for an ordinary salesman to survive a day in the modern city, as it took gladiators in the old days to fight in the arenas. In a similar vein, Wong's martial arts film shows us the danger of ordinary life.

Chungking Express, released in the same year as *Ashes of Time* (1994), returns us to the modern city, but with a difference. It manages somehow to make comedy out of characters who do not know their own desires, trying to adjust emotionally to a skewed space. The action revolves around the notorious Chungking Mansions, a dingy down-market, mall-cum-flophouse, incredibly located right in the midst of Tsimshatsui, Hong Kong's most expensive tourist area. It is a truly heterotopic space and living contradiction. It is as if all the marginal elements have now migrated to the most exclusive part of the city, existing no longer on the fringe, but as a kind of non-place or negative space at the center; standing side by side with its mainstream spaces (the world-class Peninsula Hotel is just across the road), which it represents in reverse.

After two dense and difficult films, *Chungking Express* seems to have a charming lightness. The film is split into two narrative and stylistic parts, with the fast food stall functioning as some sort of anchoring point. The first involves the cop He Qi Wu, who is being jilted by his girlfriend May, and recounts his encounter with an attractive blonde-bewigged female gangster. The second part concerns another cop, #633, who is also in the process of being thrown over by an airline flight attendant, and follows his developing relationship with the impish Ah Faye. Not only was the film shot quickly; its subject matter deals with the world of fast food, quick fixes and one night stands; in other words, with a throw-away culture, where objects, people, and relationships are all marked in one way or another with an expiry date. The films response to such a situation is to come up with what we might call throw-away images, i.e., casual looking images whose impact comes only later. For example, how many in the audience would have noticed that the three main characters in the second part of the film all made brief appearances à la Hitchcock in the first part? But they are there, in short, oblique shots. The humor, then, is that of the double-take, the delayed response. The joke is one that we laugh at only later. In this respect, Wong's comedy differs from the best known examples of Hong Kong comedy, like those made by the Hui brothers or Stephen Chiau or Jackie Chan, which rely heavily on the immediacy of slapstick or visual gags. Wong works on the very different comic principle of non-immediacy and delay, or better still, delayed immediacy. This makes the title *Chungking Express* with its connotations of speed look quite deliberately, but also gently, ironic.

One of the ways this comedy of delay works can be seen in the films playing with styles, particularly Wong's own highly distinctive film styles used in his first two films. At many points, *Chungking Express* comes close to self-parody. For example, the use in this first part of exaggerated blues and reds, of slow-motion (step-printing) techniques, of quick cutting which makes action a blur: all this recalls the style of As Tears Go By, but now used self-consciously, in a meta-stylistic way. All events therefore are mediated by a style which puts them at a distance, and reduces their seriousness, including events like the shooting of the Indians, and the foreign gangster. Similarly, part two begins with a scene that recalls the opening scene of *Days of Being Wild*: Policeman #633 smoothes his hair with his hand (like the hero of *Days* combing his hair) and orders something over the counter from Ah Faye. But instead of a quiet and dreamy heroine, we see a hyperactive Ah Faye moving to the sound of *California Dreaming* playing at high volume. #633 is no hero either, just an ordinary guy ordering a chef's salad for a girl-friend who is about to abandon him, or as she puts it, cancel his boarding pass. The jokes at this level are of the nature of in-jokes, i.e. jokes that are not perceived as such, unless we are aware of the intertextual references.

There is also a constant doubling and pairing of names, objects and people that elicits the response of the double-take. For example, May 1st is the expiry date on

a can of sardines that the foreign gangster gives to the blonde-wigged woman to remind her of her fatal deadline: the drug smuggling operation she is organizing has to be completed by that date. However, the operation goes wrong, the Indian smugglers she hires and fits out with new clothes and shoes (made by quick-delivery specialists in Chungking Mansions) disappear at the airport. She tracks them down, shoots them, and then shoots the foreign gangster. But May 1st is also the expiry date on thirty cans of pineapples that the policeman Wu has been collecting, one at a time, since April Fool's Day, when his girlfriend, named May, ditched him because he no longer reminded her of the Hollywood star of violent films, Bruce Willis. He sets May his own private deadline of May 1st to come back to him. She does not, and he eats the thirty cans of pineapples in mourning for a faithless girlfriend, at the same time that the blonde-wigged woman is shooting in revenge the faithless Indians. There are many coincidences of this kind as well as accidental collisions, like the one near the films beginning showing Wu and the blonde-wigged woman bumping into each other before they were acquainted. "At our most intimate," Wu says "we were only 0.01 cm apart"; they were closest at the moment when they didn't know each other. There is the doubling of names, May, a common name, being also the name of a another young woman working at the fast food stall, whom the stall owner recommends to Wu. When he decides to date her, as a consolation, she has already gone away with another man. So on May 1st Wu lost two Mays in one night. The double-take comes from the mis-taking of signs.

It is, therefore, not broad comedy that we find, but a comedy of details. The best illustration of this comedy of details comes in the second part of the film, in Ah Faye's sly courtship of the policeman. After the flight attendant leaves him, we see him talking to the objects in his apartment: the thin cake of soap, the ragged face towel, the fluffy white doll and so on. She also left his apartment keys in care of the fast food stall. Ah Faye uses the keys to enter the apartment when #633 is out. She cleans and tidies it up; changes his soap, towel, toothbrush; buys goldfish for the fish-tank; substitutes a yellow and black-striped toy tiger for his white doll, and Chinese black-bean mackerel for his cans of Del Monte sardines; leaves a photograph on his mirror, and so on. Still obsessed with the flight attendant, the policeman registers no surprise at the new objects, explaining them away as the result of a change in his emotional state. He does not notice Ah Faye's presence, in spite of all the clues she leaves him. Lately, I've become more observant, he says to himself, as he eats a can labeled Del Monte Sardines, which now contains black bean mackerel. It is only when he returns unexpectedly one day, catching her in his apartment, that he notices that she is there.

At one point, Ah Faye calls PC #633 a stupid man, but she says it affectionately. It seems that like the peasant-mercenary Hong Qi in Ashes of Time, only the stupid have some chance of happiness. Stupid actions produce unexpected results. For example, Wu spends a disappointing night with the blonde-wigged woman (whom he finally meets at a bar) because she just sleeps through their time together at the hotel room. But before he leaves at dawn, he takes off and polishes her high-heels shoes for her, and she unexpectedly calls him later on his beeper to wish him a happy birthday — which falls, when else?, on May 1st. Similarly, Ah Faye did not keep her appointment with #633 at the California Restaurant in Lan Kwei Fong, deciding she has to go to the real California first; but she does send him an imaginary boarding pass she had drawn for him, valid for the same time next year, which is like a kind of tacit promise to return. In these examples, there is a fleeting hint of a reciprocity that emerges from the delays.

36 ▶▶

Fallen Angels is once again a reshuffling of elements found in Wong's other films, but in such a way that it verges on being a mere exercise in style. It is indeed a stylish film that runs the risk of being too stylised. There are many references to Wong's other films, especially to Chungking Express. For example, a woman cleans up a man's apartment as a way of feeling close up him; a character becomes mute after eating an out-of-date can of pineapples; a girl dyes her hair blonde; there is a

fast food shop called Midnight Express, where a girl dressed in a flight attendant's uniform waits for her boyfriend; and so on. More than in any of the other films, the voice-over has almost completely replaced dialogue. When we do hear characters speak, it is more often to themselves or on the telephone. The result is the images now take on an even greater importance; they have a sultry seductive quality to them, hard-edged and elusive all at once. The films most interesting feature, it seems to me, is the way it manages to combine the fatalistic plot of *As Tears Go By* with the crazy comedy of *Chungking Express*. We find, therefore, two different types of stories interwined with one another, with their own set of characters.

The first story involves the hired assassin and his beautiful partner (played respectively by the photogenic Leon Lai and the even more photogenic Michelle Reis). There is a formal, arranged quality to this story, as it moves from the very first image, to its predestined end with the death of the assassin, killed on his last job. The arranged quality is underlined by the vague sense we have that we may have heard or seen what is being shown on the screen before. For example, in the opening image, shot in an exaggerated blue, of Reis and Lai facing the camera, we hear Lai's voice-over about how partners at work should not be intimate. This is the theme of proximity without intimacy that we heard before in Chungking Express. This is followed by the scene of Reis in a shiny black leatherette dress and fish-net stockings doing the house cleaning, like a kind of femme fatale Ah Faye. However, the evocation of deja vu is quite deliberate. It suggests the fatality of the already happened that leaves no way out. Just as the assassin is caught in all the doomed images of the genre, so the woman is doubly caught in the stereotyped images of genre and gender, of femme fatale and house wife. Images may be abstract but they are nonetheless real.

Once again, it is in terms of the erotic that the contradictions of the situation are most painfully felt. On the one hand, the woman wants to know the assassin, to feel close to him. She goes through his garbage to find out from what he does not want, what he does want; a painstaking hermeneutics of waste. She goes to the bar that she knows he frequents and sits at his table, to feel close to him. On the other hand, she reflects, knowing too much about a person can be boring. I am realistic, she says in a voice-over, I know how to make myself happy. This means, we find out almost immediately, retreating to auto-eroticism; that is to say, to phantasies and melancholic images without an object. The masturbation scene that follows (there is another one later in the film) is itself an image, shot beautifully as fragments of the body, distorted through carefully chosen camera angles, in vivid colour and with suggestive music in the background. Eroticism in the film is joyless, suspended between boredom and melancholy. For all the fallen angels that inhabit this space, the right distance from the real is never found.

Counterpointing and crazing a little the formal stylishness and frozen images of the first story are all those other stories of ordinary lives that accompany it. They seem accidental, idiosyncratic, a little absurd, like the characters they introduce. There is, for example, Leon's accidental meeting after a dangerous mission with a blustering old school mate on a minibus, who, of all things, ends up trying to sell the assassin an insurance policy. Then there are all those kooks and wierdos of the night, like the girl with dyed blonde hair that Leon meets at an empty all-night Macdonald's. She snuggles up to him and asks, "Is this seat taken?" She dyes her hair, she says, to be remembered. Or there is the girl talking to someone she thought was her boyfriend on the telephone, who announces that he wants to get married — to someone else; apparently to another girl with blonde hair whom she spends the rest of the night desparately seeking, accompanied by a mute boy. All these pathetic creatures have the same simple desire — to be remembered, to be recognised, to be wanted. But all of them have the same fate: they are forgotten or abandoned. The girl with blonde hair tells Leon that in fact they knew each other before when she had long hair — but he had already forgotten.

The only happy person in this desparate company is the mute boy, mute like the classic clown. He is an ex-convict, has few friends and no job. He decides therefore,

by the application of an unconventional logic, to be his own boss. But he has no capital either, so he breaks into other people's business establishments after hours, and runs them as his own. No wonder he gets into trouble with the law. There is a funny sequence where we see him run, by turns, a butcher shop, a laundry, a grocery store, a hairdressing salon and an ice-cream van. And he literally forces his business on his customers, particularly on a bearded man who has the misfortune to run into him everywhere. On different occasions, the man is forced to have a shampoo, or a shave, or a huge portion of baked-Alaska ice cream. Like the classic clowns, particularly Charlie Chaplin, the mute boy is not a rebel or a critic of capitalist society. He is merely its negative representation, comically showing how it works non-stop, and its practice of the hard sell.

There is an interesting contrast too that can be drawn between the erotic relation of Michelle and Leon, and the affective relation of the mute boy and his father, when we consider the ways these relations are visually represented. The first is represented in some of the most seductive images of the Hong Kong cinema, the second through the clumsiness of home video. The mute boy videos his father, in a gesture of affection, in all kinds of awkward situations: when he is at work (in Chungking Mansions), dealing with difficult customers; when he is at home in the kitchen, in the bathroom, or in bed sleeping. These video images, in a film of carefully made images, have a frail, unmade quality to them. The father dies soon after the video is made; but watching it again, in the father's absence, the son can feel happy.

It is also the elusiveness of happiness and other migrancies that Wong Kar Wai returns to in his latest film, *Happy Together*. In this film, the device of the voice-over, a Wong trade-mark, while still present, is used sparingly. We find dialogue again, even if it is of characters arguing. There is a very graphic homosexual scene between the two main characters Ho Po-wing and Lai Yin-fai at the beginning of the film, but after that they spend most of the time fighting and frustrated with each other. They left Hong Kong and drifted to Argentina in order to start over again. But just as their nomadic adventures take many wrong turns (they either lose their way looking for the Iguazu Waterfall, or go walking when the weather is too cold), so their erotic relations run into many obstacles, as passion turns into boredom or suspicion. The nomadic and the erotic have something in common: neither can avoid disappointment.

One of the most important images in the film is a banal object, a kitschy lamp that Ho and Lai bought when they were happy together. The revolving lampshade shows a picture of Iguazu Waterfalls, a South American equivalent of Niagara Falls. Ho and Lai never made it to Iguazu. The first time they tried, they lost their way, and we are given a first image of Iguazu, caught in slow motion, with La Paloma playing on the sound track: an imagined Iguazu. Later in the film, we are given a very similar image of Iguazu, seen through the eyes of Lai, but now accompanied by the music of the sleazy tango bars of Buenos Aires. Lai is now there alone, having broken up with Ho. These paired shots of Iguazu suggest how images of happiness can turn into their opposite, just as the phrase that Ho likes to use, "to start over again," can signify both the beginning or the end of a relationship.

Something of these ambiguities also comes out of the spatial experience of the film; for example, in the reversability of Hong Kong and Buenos Aires, of home and elsewhere. At one level, Buenos Aires is the antipode of Hong Kong, the other side of the world. Day in one place is night in the other, summer is winter, and so on. There is even a Georg Baselitz-like shot late in the film of Hong Kong upside down. But this spatial symmetry of opposites soon breaks down into repetition and seriality. Buenos Aires looks very much like the Hong Kong of Wong's other films, presented in fragments and in medium shots. Both cities take on the quality of what Gilles Deleuze has called any-space-whatever: ordinary spaces which have somehow lost their particularity and system of interconnectedness. In this sense then, Hong Kong and Buenos Aires are repetitions of each other. This ambiguous

interchangability is also a part of the experience of what is called globalism, and one important implication of global space is that home loses its specificity, and homelessness its pathos. As Lai says at one point late in the film, what goes around, comes around. In such a space, where would the end of the world be, that the film's third character, the Taiwanese Zhang, wants to see? It would not be a terminal point, but the beginning of a journey home, which we now know is just another elsewhere.

In *Happy Together* then, even more centrally then in Wong's other films, spatial experiences parallel and counterpoint affective experience, the nomadic and the erotic arrive at similar conclusions. Yet there is one last contradiction that challenges these conclusions. If the search for happiness is, as we are suggesting, like looking for the end of the world, i.e. an impossibility, yet in the film, the characters continue to do both in spite of repeated disappointments. In one sense then the title *Happy Together* is ironic. It suggests that in the space described by the film, love goes together with disappointment, and this is as true of homosexual love as of any other kind. Ho and Lai cannot be happy and together at the same time. Yet in another sense, the title is not ironic at all, because the characters remain eudaemonists, believers in happiness, always ready to come together and, in the key phrase of the film, start over again. They are what I will call serial eudaemonists. Wong's films are filled with such characters who, without the help of psychoanalysis, have learned how to turn neurotic pain into ordinary unhappiness.

A DIALOGUE WITH WONG KAR-WAI
CUTTING BETWEEN TIME AND TWO CITIES

*TIME: June, 1995
*PLACE: Westwood Plaza Hotel, Los Angeles
(Wong Kar-Wai and I are here for the American premiere of *Chungking Express*, part of the program at the Los Angeles Asian-Pacific Film and Video Festival. Quentin Tarantino, whose company is going to release the film in America next year, presented the film at the Melnitz Theater, UCLA, two nights ago.)

*NGAI: Good, this is a serious dialogue. Where do we begin?

*WONG: You tell me.

*Let's try Quentin Tarantino, the guy who is responsible for introducing the works of Wong Kar-Wai to the American cinema-going public.

*The most-quoted guy in Los Angeles in 1995. And?

*Try and t ell us "How Quentin Tarantino Became A Fan of Wong Kar-Wai".

*Tarantino strikes me as someone who really enjoys movies. I think he sees just about anything, and is interested in everything he sees. Some people love to tell others that they want to direct films, whereas Tarantino actually does it — his satisfaction comes from the process of making a movie, not the idea of making it. For me, some filmmakers may be working in different places on totally different things, but when their works come out, the spirit can be very much alike. Just like when Tarantino sees the work of Takeshi Kitano, he understands what Kitano is doing; he sees the work of Wong Kar-Wai, he understands what I am doing. We may not be working on the same thing, but somehow we manage to find this comprehension in the air, like students from the same class, reunited after years of separation. Look at it in another way, we are different from those directors before us. Directors in the old days had lots to discover: the movie world was fresh then. It was an undiscovered space, waiting for people to explore. Now we have reached an age of recycling. Our generation gets to see lots of movies, and takes these movies to heart; and we knock them down and start reconstructing. It is like going to the same supermarket where we are all faced with the same stock, we make an effort to cook up something new. And we get fun out of doing that.

* Interview June, 1995. Westwood Plaza Hotel, Los Angeles.
** Interview August, 1997. Park Hyatt Hotel, Tokyo.

**TIME: August, 1997
**PLACE: Park Hyatt Hotel, Tokyo
(A promotional tour for the September release of *Happy Together* brings Wong Kar-Wai here. I am on holiday, at the same time preparing for this dialogue. Several hours ago, by arrangement of *BRUTUS* magazine, Wong Kar-Wai and Takeshi Kitano were interviewing each other. Some days later, Takeshi will be bringing *Hara-bi* to the Venice Film Festival.)

**Talking about Takeshi Kitano, during the interview, he made a lovely remark, saying that when he looked at your works, he thought you must have come from a good family, and were well brought up, whereas he himself had been a street kid, and that shows in his works. It was like saying that you are the Good Guy and he is the Bad Boy.*

**I would much prefer being the Bad Boy — things are always more interesting for Bad Boys. When I saw *Kids Return*, I felt a deep nostalgia at the opening sequence, in which two kids are doing some talk show in a small theatre and the camera moves around the very confined backstage. After I first came to Hong Kong from Shanghai, I was living in Tsimshatsui, an area frequented by girls who were generally known as Suzy Wong — girls who worked in the bars entertaining sailors arriving on those battleships. There were lots of bars and clubs in that area which was my world at that time, and I was very much attracted to this sort of sleazy establishment. I had no problem identifying with street kids.

**So far, all your works have depicted nothing but sleazy establishments of both the modern and ancient worlds. It is as if your heart only goes to underdogs.*

**I always find underdogs more interesting, more worthy of my attention. Anyway, theirs was the world I came from, so I have a feeling for them. Plus, I know I can handle this world.

**It would be interesting to see your work move towards high society.*

**Nobody can outdo Visconti when it comes to high society. He did it best. But then again, twentieth century Italian high society has traditionally offered lots more possibilities.

**Are you a nostalgic person? Your obsession, or near obsession, with things past is remarkable. The beautiful, or beautifully painful, memory of the days gone — hence the title* Days of Being Wild;

a past history that cannot be rewritten but is carried around buried deep inside the self, skillfully demonstrated in Ashes of Time; *the question of mobility versus immobility — an indecision involving both external and internal journey — which has always been a key motif of your works but became full-blown in* Chungking Express *and* Fallen Angels, *and which was carried forward to* Happy Together; *the dream of flying, versus the self-acknowledgement of one's uncorrectable inability to do so, which can clearly be read as the loss of innocence…*

**I guess I find this "loss of innocence" thing deeply intriguing. Time, to me, forever brings a loss of innocence. As you go through time, you are bound to look back with hindsight, you begin to reminisce about things that you dreamed about doing but didn't get to do, you begin to wonder what would have happened on that particular day if you had taken a different turn on the road. You have no answer for sure, but you are distressed by the possible outcome of things you didn't do. You cannot help but regret.

Time and again you have declared that you are a sixties romantic: the sun was brighter then, the streets more friendly, with radiobroadcast floating in the air.

*I didn't think much about it at the time of *Days of Being Wild*. It wasn't until I began working on *Fallen Angels* that I became conscious of trying to capture time. My way of working is generally to first establish a world or an environment, say Tsimshatsui or Central (both in the case of *Chungking Express*); then to try everything to stick to this area. Like, once after I decided on Tsimshatsui, I went around the area looking for things that I want ed to shoot — I refused to look into other areas. For *Fallen Angels*, originally I thought of going back to Tsimshatsui to do more of the same, but I then discovered I had more or less explored the area enough for me to move on to something else. So I looked around for something different, and one day I was in Wanchai. The Wanchai area, basically, is a bizarre mixture of modern buildings and some very old ones. Small newspaper shops in building entrances, laundries that date back to the fifties and sixties, Chinese restaurants that saw better days years ago… and I realized these things would disappear from our world very soon. You come shooting here today, tomorrow it could be gone. Today, on TV, they still sometimes show Cantonese features made thirty, forty years ago, and we are deeply attracted by those streets that look totally

42 ▶▶

different today. Most people don't work like that, but things like geographical factors affect me a lot. It was like I was trying to preserve something from perishing.

Mourning before the death.

*Maybe. With *Days of Being Wild*, it was more a reinvention of the disappeared world; with *Fallen Angels*, it is an attempt to seal some of the existing images onto the negative, while they are still there.

**Geographical factors traditionally play an important role in your works. In* As Tears Go By, *the protagonist's romantic object comes from an outlying island, signifying an uncorrupted force which doubles as the sanctuary. Then there is the Philippines in* Days of Being Wild, *a primitive, unknown origin, full of danger for the bird with no legs. With* Ashes of Time, *the desert serves as the graveyard for the man who violated his love and then chose to stay alive as one of the living dead — the greatest revenge on the woman. Then of course we have Argentina as "the other side of the world" in* Happy Together — *a world waiting for the protagonist's awakening.*

**It is probable that this has everything to do with my transplant from Shanghai to Hong Kong at the age of 5. When I got there, I spoke nothing but Shanghainese, whereas Cantonese was, and still is, the local dialect. For some time, I was totally alienated, and it was like the biggest nightmare of my life. It might not be conscious, but certainly I have an intense feeling for geographical upheavals.

**That explains everything. Characters in* Days of Being Wild, *becoming friends only because, as kids, they were neighbors; characters drifting in and out of other people's homes and hotels, in both* Chungking Express *and* Fallen Angels, *to which we may add* Happy Together…

**I believe geographical accessability is a deciding factor for human relationships. We don't really choose our friends, people who are around us become our friends.

**Right from day one, you have stuck to the theme of "home": the longing to know what a home is like; the availability of a home as a sanctuary protecting you from the outside world; the idea that a house is not a home; that a pied-à-terre is nothing but a pied-à-terre… This is a recurring theme that you keep going back to.*

**I did not have a particularly happy childhood. So "home" is a magic word for me. Of course, becoming a father a few years back made me even more conscious of this.

**I find the father-and-son sequence in* Fallen Angels *very moving — I am actually convinced that that sequence is about the most personal bit to have come from Wong Kar-Wai to date. Care to talk about it?*

**It was very difficult for me. Making that.

**And then you went back to the father figure in* Happy Together *— a role that apparently symbolizes redemption.*

**No, not redemption. It is more like yielding to understanding. The need to be understood by someone you care for.

Tarantino says that there are two kinds of scripts that he writes: those he writes for others to direct, and those he writes for himself.

*Definitely. I started as a scriptwriter, and learned the rules of the game very early on. To be a scriptwriter, you have to know exactly what the others want from you — the others being the director, the producer and the boss. Directors can be lousy liars at times: what they say is one thing, what they really want is another. Very often, the scriptwriter is stuck between the director and the boss — the two may have very different ideas regarding the same project that they hired you for. So you try hard to serve these different needs. Doing a script for yourself is another story — a simpler story but at the same time more complicated. At times I would sit in front of an old script that I had written and wonder how I would do it if I were the director. Some stories, if I were to direct them, would flow in another direction. And then I became a director, and I am often stuck with this enormous pain of writing my own script. At those times I would ask myself: Why can't you just write it as if writing for somebody else? Just do a simple story? But I guess some things you just can't help.

What is the essential difference between the two types of script?

*Scripts that I do for others are often easy to read. From beginning to end, a scene gives the feeling of a scene. When I do it for myself, I can't do scenes like that — I start to get concerned about where the camera is, how the actors move… things like that. These things can't be put into the script, because once you put them in, the rhythm is gone. And rhythm is the essence of a script: to help the director and actors

to see and feel the rhythm of the movie. When I do a script for myself, I don't see rhythm, I see visuals. A visual script is a very difficult script to direct. In order to do a good script, you should stay away from describing the visual. I always advise new scriptwriters not to write in the camera: a close-up here, a long shot there... It ties the director down.

I always imagined some directors might find camera movements helpful.

*Never. No. Also, it has everything to do with the rhythm that I talked about. A script should always include the crucial information, but nothing else: time, place, characters and dialogue, plus the necessary movement. That is that.

I have lots of fun reading Tarantino's scripts. It's obvious that the guy really enjoyed writing them. I can just imagine him sitting in front of his typewriter, or word processor, giggling away.

*I doubt if he giggles too much these days. When everyone is keeping an eye on you and your forthcoming project, it's kind of hard to giggle.

In Hong Kong, there has always been lots of gossip concerning Wong Kar-Wai's

movies and the script — "is there a script or isn't there": the existence (or non-existence) of the mysterious script that forever puts the production on hold.

*The problem is that I am my own scriptwriter and so between the scriptwriter and the director I change my mind easily. Too easily, probably. There are times I tell myself that just sticking to the original idea would be easier for all parties, that changing one scene could have a domino effect and cause further changes. But being the director, I generally opt for those changes, in view of a better result. Also, once shooting has started, changes always help to better fit the role to the actor. You say to yourself, a slight change won't matter. So changes take place here and there. Then these changes accumulate into chaos, waiting for you to clear it up.

So you are saying that a director who writes his own script is better than a director who doesn't, because he can change the script to fit the actors, and so head for a better result?

*It's a matter of practice. My habit is to develop the script according to actors. I generally start writing after I have the actors in mind. Other people usually find a story they want to do, get a scriptwriter to write it down, then look around for their actors. In that case, they don't need to alter the script to fit the actors.

Wasn't As Tears Go By done in that way?

*Lots of changes have gone into As Tears Go By before shooting started. But I do agree directors who know how to do scripts have an edge.

Know how, but don't necessarily do it themselves?

* Don't necessarily do it themselves. I always think there must be people who can do better script than I can. I have always hoped that I could get someone who could do script for me, but over the years I still haven't found that person. Of course this is my problem, not a matter of quality. Sometimes when I see a movie, I ask myself: if I were to direct it, how would I do it?

Back to the question about the scriptwriter serving the director.

*That involves experience. When you are new to the business, you keep suggesting "let's do this, let's do that"; and as you become more accustomed to the industry, you begin to understand the reason why people are doing things the way they are. You begin to know more about distribution, more about personal relationships. You stop telling people "let's do this, let's do that," because now you have a grasp on how things are being run, what the rules are. You serve this end. The problem with some scriptwriters is that they are not generous enough, meaning that they tend to tie the director down. Neil Simon is not a generous scriptwriter in the sense that no director can ever escape from his scripts.

45 ▶▶

In your case, you have about broken every rule as a director.

*Changes happen all the time. I have been in the movie industry for many years, and I have yet to witness one project that sticks to the original script from beginning till end.

**Typically all your works have two versions of synopsis: before and after. The two versions tell two different stories.*

**You know, I get bored easily, and executing an idea without allowing any change can be pretty boring. In the actual process of making the film, the story

evolves — something that seems so natural to me that I don't even notice. When I arrived in Argentina, I was equipped with my synopsis of *Happy Together*, and I thought that was all I needed. When I was there, I began to look closely at what I had and, eventually, I ended up with another story that looks more like the sequel to my original one. And then, of course, further changes happen in the editing room.

**That is one of the reasons why monologue plays such an important role in your works: it puts the story together. The use of monologue provides you with a much larger space in the editing room — you're freed from the footage you see on the screen, and you are able to lead the story in any direction as you see fit.*

**I always think monologue a very interesting device. It can be something happening inside a character, an internal communication, an observation; it can be something directed towards the audience, a confession or an excuse that the character wants to make; or it can be a reminder of something which has happened, or even a lie. The audience has to decide which is which. Of course, monologue is always helpful in providing information that we don't get to see on screen.

**Which reminds me, the use of monologue in* Ashes of Time *is a disaster for a western audience. I mean, recognizing those faces is already a trying task for people who are not familiar with the actors, but having three or four voices coming up without any apparent clue as to which voice belongs to whom can be a nightmare.*

**That one was a serious lesson. The problem did not come to my mind until it was too late. I was doomed with no way out. So when it came to *Happy Together*, I had to be extremely careful with my way of placing monologues.

**Would you agree that people are afraid of trying anything new in Hong Kong?*

*One has to understand the nature of Hong Kong's movie industry before one can talk about trying anything new. The nature of the local industry is for export. Most films are independent productions, which means they have to get some overseas sales before the budget is secure enough for the production to begin. But how do you get overseas sales before the shooting even begins? You have to sell relying on either the actors or the genre — anything that is tried and proven. If something sells like a hotcake, everybody tries to make a copy as soon as possible, hoping they are not too late. The situation doesn't allow you to sit and write about something you really want to write about, and then carry it around trying to sell it. Tarantino could have been sitting inside the videoshop for many years before he came up with those scripts. But the local industry wouldn't allow that.

That makes your route even more amazing. I am inclined to think that you were very conscious in attempting to tackle the whole set of rules within the industry, in breaking away from the normal practice. Before As Tears Go By, *you were already familiar enough with the system and were forming your own idea of how it could have functioned otherwise; or at least you were not afraid to toy with the system, to see how far it could be stretched. You wanted to find a way you could break away from the system while at the same time working within the industry. After your first film, you established your own little space as a base, and from there the show became yours.*

*And?

And... I don't know. What really baffles me is: Was there any other Wong Kar-Wais in our industry before you, who just died out before anyone even heard of those names?

Or, are you the only one in the whole history of our industry who made such an attempt and succeeded? I hope I don't sound as if I am not taking your artistic talent into account, I just really want to dig into Wong Kar-Wai's systematic attack on the existing Hong Kong system.

*To you, maybe I am the courageous man. To me, it is a totally different story. From day one, it has been like striving to survive. I have no idea how I entered into this, but ever since I have been striving to survive.

You must have been dying to become a director in your scriptwriting stage.

*After I became a director I strove to survive.

Is this "striving to survive" occasional, or compulsive?

*As Tears Go By *was smooth enough; because of it, I was given the chance to make* Days of Being Wild. *You know the controversy that came after* Days of Being Wild *was released. After that, my feeling has always been like a single pair of hands facing an entire army — you don't know when you're going to perish.

*Evidently you haven't.

*My biggest problem is that I don't ever get time to slow down. At some stage, ideally, I should be able to take my time, to reflect on where I want to go, what I want to do. As things are, it is more like: don't think, grab whatever chance, and do it. People always ask me how come my style is always changing. You can say that most of the time I don't even know where I am heading. Rushing ahead without seeing.

**When Fallen Angels came out, I was of the opinion that the film, together with the four previous works, marked the first stage of your career.

**I never look at it that way. To me, all my works are really like different episodes of one movie.

**My argument, of course, is that it is very unlikely for a creative person to declare: Look, I'm moving into another stage. Things like that generally do not happen on a conscious level. After As Tears Go By, you did Days of Being Wild, which is nothing less than a thesis on "The Dreamfilm of Wong Kar-Wai". Then you moved straight onto Ashes of Time, beyond doubt your most ambitious project to date, which was followed by the stylistically refreshing Chungking Express. For me, Fallen Angels has always been like a Wong Kar-Wai sampler, a showcase. I always recommend that people, who have never seen Wong Kar-Wai before, begin with this film, as it has all the key elements of your previous works in it, and is an ideal introductory piece. In terms of your career, Fallen Angels is a piece that marks an end, waiting for something to happen.

**It is possible that through Fallen Angels, I was reinforcing my own belief in many things. When I was shooting the film, lots of things were happening within the local film industry, and hearing those things got me quite upset. It was nothing personal, but I felt this frustration inside me.

**This frustration is well reflected in the killer (Leon Lai), with lines like, "I'm tired of pulling bullets out of my body", and his general attitude towards his surroundings. After that, we have the catch phase, "Let's start over," in Happy Together.

**You know the line really didn't mean anything else to me when it first popped up, apart from its obvious meaning referring to the relationship. Only much later was I able to read the underlying meaning: a reference to the sentiments of a person

who has been trapped in the 1997 situation for fourteen years. If I had read the underlying meaning much earlier on, I might have decided against using the line, thinking it too obvious.

**I am happy to report that, on top of the political undertones, the line perfectly fits my scenario: the first film of a new stage in your career. These days, after* Happy Together, *are you still rushing ahead without seeing? People are already asking about* Summer in Beijing, *your next project.*

**Looks like the current situation won't allow me the luxury of reflection. You come up with a new work, and distributors all over the world want you to go there to help promote the work, and before the round is finished people begin asking about your next project.

**The cycle never ends.*

**The trouble is that you are glad the cycle is repeated, because you know you're still in demand. This is where the dilemma lies.

Back to controversy. The controversy you caused in Hong Kong is phenomenal.

*Sure. Because the whole thing has gone against what our whole industry collectively believes in. Making a film that doesn't sell is already bad enough; a commercially failed filmmaker getting more work is even worse; and on top of that a whole bunch of people are telling everyone that this filmmaker has made some very, very good films… This is about as controversial as you can get.

How did you make that happen?

*You see, *Days of Being Wild* is a very attractive film.

You're telling me that?

*I mean from an investor's point of view. The same with *Ashes of Time*: the potential popularity that the title promises, the cast. There is this chemistry that appeals to an investor, that draws them like honey drawing a bee.

But the honey was just an illusion, in the end it was not honored.

*Objectively speaking, true. Investment is always a bet, I don't think there is such a thing as sure-win. As a director, I can never tell how my film is going to turn out — the uncertainty is infinite. I have never known how to go out and decide on making a film that is going to sell. I am a bit of a punter. I have always thought there is something of a punter inside me. But I only like to bet on things that I have some control over. Like in Black Jack.

Recently, I saw As Tears Go By *again, and I realized there was a certain prettiness to the film that one doesn't get to see in any of your other works. A prettiness that seems to come from William Chang, the production designer; a prettiness that is strangely teen-idolish. Of course all your other works are visually impressive, but not in such a way.*

*I can see what you mean. Looking back, I would agree the aesthetics of *As Tears Go By* are a bit too… fresh. Some things got beautified.

In terms of prettiness, it was downhill all the way after that film.

*Of course you have noticed all my films have got more and more worn and torn. But again, they all come from the same William. I guess we moved on a bit after our first film together.

*Could it be that you were a bit overwhelmed by him at that time — bearing in mind *As Tears Go By* was your directorial debut?*

*I have known William since well before *As Tears Go By*, and we mutually trust each other. With us, it is more like we are going to get something done and it really doesn't matter if it is done by him or by me. We think alike. Since *Ashes of Time*, William has been the film editor of my works, as well as the production designer; we work perfectly happy together.

*As a work by Wong Kar-Wai, *As Tears Go By* is unique in it that the film has a linear narrative line — something not to be seen thereafter.*

*At that stage, I still believed in telling a story with appropriate this and appropriate that, observing the recipe closely.

And you were comfortable with the recipe?

*Before *As Tears Go By*, I spent years on the script of *Final Victory*. One day after I handed in my script, the guys said to me: "But the triads don't talk like that." That stuck. From then on, I decided "characters" should come before anything else: when you get hold of your characters, you get hold of lots of other things. Consequently, my works tend to become "character films" more than "story films". Then I was concerned that a film with some clear

characters in it, told in simple narrative form, could be very predictable, thus unappealing. I tried to get around it Then came Days of Being Wild. One day, I discovered I could chop those happenings into small pieces, and rearrange them with numerous possibilities… It was like I saw the light.

**With Happy Together, *we witness a return to the more traditional linear narrative structure. Does that mean you have seen new light?*

**When the rough cut for *Happy Together* was finished in the editing room, I saw nearly three hours of footage. I looked and looked, and I decided that I didn't need an "epic", I needed a simple story told in a regular ninety-minute format. So I chopped away three female side-characters and concentrated on the men. One lesson I learned from *Ashes of Time* was that I tried to tell too much with too little space, and it ended up becoming too stylish in story-telling, and that was not my intention. I originally intended to tell a daily life story of a man who buried himself in the desert. And this time I wanted to steer away from any distraction, but stick close to the relationship between these men. You can say that after examining different recipes,

maybe I wanted to try my hand at consumé.

You were never in the dark again after Days of Being Wild.

*All through the making of *As Tears Go By*, I had no clue what Andy Lau's role was after — What did he want? Was he tired of the triad life, or was the girl just a passing stage for him? All of this, I cannot answer. But now, of course, I can say that there are people who are like that, having no clear idea what they themselves want, just drifting about.

Sounds like that role was very much parallel to your own self at that particular time.

*Certainly.

**I think Andy Lau's role in *As Tears Go By* serves something like an original mould. In your following works, lots of characters can be traced back to this role.*

**Really? How?

**The role has two sides confronting each other: his committed care for his "little bro" (played by Jacky Cheung) who about sums up his past history as a triad member, and his love for this girl (played by Maggie

Cheung) that symbolizes a new life after triad society. Compromise between the two forces seems out of the question, bearing in mind that this fraternal commitment never gets to meet the romantic impersonation in the film. Guilt, suffering are juxtaposed with hope, struggle. This quality is divided up between So Lai-Chuen (Maggie Cheung) and MimiLulu (Carina Lau) in Days of Being Wild: the former with a capacity for suffering, the latter a will to struggle. Then of course guilt, suffering, hope, survival got split into various characters in Ashes of Time, these characters come like a parade into the desert to tempt Au-Yeung Fung back into mobility or further down into immobility, as Thomas of Beckett was tempted. The example goes on. And then these qualities are reunited in Lai Yiu-Fai (Tony Leung) of Happy Together.

**After *Happy Together* came out, people always asked which character I can identify with, and my answer is: there is always part of me in every character I create, they all have something I can identify with, a human side that I cherish. I have lots of sympathy for Ho Po-Wing (Leslie Cheung) because, at the end of the day, he is the loser. Unlike Lai Yiu-Fai, Po-Wing has neither the capacity to suffer, nor a will to struggle — it is more like an animal instinct that keeps him more or less intact on the streets. As for Chang (Chang Chun), we all know we don't have to worry for him — he's a kid who knows pretty well where he is heading.

***I was about to say Chang is probably the most positive character coming out of your world to date, whereas the dark side of Lai Yiu-Fai is nearly Fassbinderian. You always make a big point of being able to identify with all your characters.*

**Naturally. I do not believe in writing a character that I do not care about. The audience would know immediately. The audience would think: if the director/scriptwriter does not care about this character, why should we? You have to love all your characters for them to come alive.

*Back to Days of Being Wild. *By that time, you already knew what you wanted as a director?*

*It has been very difficult. I knew there was something that I wanted, I was not at all sure how to get at it.

**But there was this attempt hanging in the air. Like the man who thought he was going to fly?*

*Something like that. An itch to try my hand.

*You have come a long way since, how do you see Days of Being Wild now?

*Now of course I can see problems with the film. The women are all better portrayed than the men, more substantial. And the overall control has been slightly excessive. I guess what is important, what means so much to me, is that I did it at that time. Or else I probably wouldn't have done it at all. It was fortunate that I got the chance, the courage, and blind faith all together in myself at the right moment.

*Concluding the whole experience of making Days of Being Wild, which would you site as the most memorable?

*Shooting on location in the Philippines was memorable. Basically, the whole crew had gone nuts by that time — it was the final stage of shooting and we were rushing to finish the film for Christmas release. I have no idea how many hours we spent on location, I just remember I felt like I had entered another state of life. What the film now contains is only a small part of what we did in the Philippines: we shot a whole subplot there about what happened to the biological parents of Yuddy (Leslie Cheung).

What was so funny was that on the morning of arrival, we found out that the place looked totally different from what we had seen on photo, and I had to keep telling myself that I didn't have any other choice, that the film had to be finished on time… Basically I was hypnotizing myself from fright. And when night fell, I looked over and saw the Philippine crew sitting there having a meal, while we were setting the light for the next scene. For a split second, I was convinced that this was a world that existed in the thirties in the Philippines, that a world created by me was actually happening around me. I knew I was going crazy then.

*Nothing ever came close after that? Not even Ashes of Time? All those long months spent in that godforsaken wasteland in remote parts of China?

*We can safely say that Days of Being Wild is, and will remain, the most personal film of all my works. I threw my whole self in. After that, I learned to control myself. I would never again forget that I am just making a film.

**How about Happy Together?

**We originally planned to have a six-week shoot in Argentina; in the end, we

spent over three months there. There had been long waits in between. Strangely enough, my Argentine experience is really not about the film, but about myself. I learned the feeling of living in a country where TV, radio and newspapers stop existing for you because of the language barrier, the feeling of idling in time with nothing happening, the feeling that I imagine to be the feeling of an exile. I suspect the whole thing was very existential, though apparently nobody uses this word anymore.

*Originally, Days of Being Wild was supposed to be a two-part movie, and there was to be a director's cut after the commercial release of the two-part work.

*Looks like this is a wish unlikely to materialize.

*But loads of footage was shot at that time.

*It should still be lying somewhere in storage.

*It was fantastic footage. Tony Leung, as one may expect, is mesmerizing.

*Memory acquires a rosy hue. I have some very romantic memories regarding the film and the unused footage.

*A simple question: in conclusion, what have you gained from Days of Being Wild? I mean apart from the obvious.

*Chris Doyle and I had some very strong exchanges of opinion during the shooting. When it was over, he told me the whole experience actually taught him that he could achieve what he set out to do with cinematography. For me, I guess I can say the same. Through the process, I learned that I can handle things that have been created inside my mind, that I am capable of materializing those ideas. Days of Being Wild, for me, was a rather ambitious project to undertake at that time — the structure, the narrative line that I had chosen… My question for myself was really: as a director, am I capable of honoring what I have in mind as a scriptwriter? In the end, I surpassed myself. I was happy that I didn't simply turn my script into a movie; in the process, Wong Kar-Wai, the director, managed to add something into the work.

*In one of our early interviews, we talked about pressure. You said pressure can be external, applied by the outside world, or it can be internal, coming from your inner self. How do you see pressure now?

*You know you have to survive, hence pressure. You know you have to be very careful with the commercial side of your works. Size is a deciding factor. Take *Ashes of Time*, for example, it was such a big-budget production that you knew from the beginning that you needed to please a wide audience for the box to break even. But then you didn't really want to make a film to please. So there arose this tightrope situation which I was stuck with. Logically enough, *Chungking Express* came at a time when I much needed a change of air: it was small-budget, it was fun.

*Fun comes out very obviously in the film.

*The crucial bit is that a big difference lies between making something that you know is going to please yourself and the market, and making something that you know you want to make, but have no idea how the market is going to receive.

**After Cannes, after your being awarded Best Director there, did your view on pressure change?*

**I guess you still have to survive, so I can't see pressure suddenly disappearing into the air. In a way, I am glad that *Happy Together* was awarded Best Director but not the Palme d'Or. The Palme d'Or would have created lots of expectations on my next project, people would have been very curious about what I was going to do after a Palme d'Or. From a director's point, Best Director gives me more space to work in, with less attention.

It amazes me enormously that Chungking Express *should be the work that placed you squarely on the international map. I have always seen that work as a matter of convenience, meaning it was totally unplanned, that you just had to rush off from the postproduction of* Ashes of Time *at that time, and engage yourself in some more refreshing exercise. And I dare say the result turned out to be something you never expected, certainly not on that scale.*

*For some reason, I just found myself desperately in need of working on something else, something to unleash my… frustration? Or maybe I was in need of a recharge — *Ashes of Time* drained me. Granted, *Chungking Express* was not a planned move. On the first shooting day, I knew about nothing of what I was going to do.

An impromptu exercise that turned out to be a highlight of your career.

*It was all very subconscious. Naturally, the making of *Chungking Express* was very

relaxed. I guess pleasantry always has an advantage. People are generally attracted to pleasant things, pleasant people. People all over the world are just the same. As you grow old, you tend to get less uptight. You become more relaxed.

**With Chungking Express, *we can see another case of characters being parallel to your real life situation: the Golden Wig Woman (Brigitte Lin) and Faye. One woman who is desperate to run away from the situation but finds herself paralyzed, another woman who is free to go anywhere but instead gleefully indulges herself in a stranger's home. One side of the coin was resentment, the other longing. Your sentiment towards the film industry at the time was thus perfectly captured. Is* Happy Together *relaxed?*

**You know, every time we visit other countries, we people from Hong Kong have been forced to answer the question of 1997 for many, many years. It got pretty boring, repeating your opinion every ten minutes. One of the reasons I chose Argentina was that it is on the other side of the world, and I thought by going there, I would be able to stay away from 1997. But then, as you must understand, once you consciously try to stay away from something or to forget

something, you will never succeed. That something is bound to be hanging in the air, haunting you.

*Since Days of Being Wild, *you have been essentially working with the same crew. You only like to work with people that you are familiar with?*

*There are pros and cons working with people that you are familiar with. On the one hand, lots of things go without saying, communication is just one look away; on the other hand, you have to make double efforts to ensure that you are coming up with new ideas, not just repeating some tried and proven tricks. So while I keep William Chang and Chris Doyle as my Production Designer and Director of Cinematography, I try to bring in new actors as a stimulant. The same crew working with different actors on different subject matters, it would be ideal.

But certainly people working with you have their own strong and weak points, like you yourself have strong and weak points.

*That doesn't matter. Granted, different cinematographers develop different styles. The important thing is to bring out each one's strong point to achieve what you have in mind. Take *Days of Being Wild, *for example, Chris's lighting makes the film, but his camera work has problems. Or *Chungking Express*, the style of the film was actually established between Lau Wai-Keung and me when Lau was doing the cinematography for the first part; so when Chris came in, he just had to extend that style. To me, *Ashes of Time* was a big test for Chris: he has always been a lighting man, good at working indoors, within the city; so when he was transplanted to a desert, with only the sun and clouds to work on, that was a challenge. New things came out like that.

**So, visually, lots of the things that we see on screen are not part of the pre-production design, but are more make-do with the available?

**You know, William has a very defined taste for colors and anything visual. So when we were on location scouting around Buenos Aires, he was at first reluctant to succumb to part of the city's loud and slightly gaudy atmosphere, but in the end he turned around and transformed those qualities into something that suited him, by mixing them with his own aesthetic sensitivity. People are always very curious about the visual effects in my works. The not so romantic truth is that lots of those

effects are in reality results of circumstantial consideration: if there is not enough space for camera maneuvering, replace the regular lens with a wide-angle lens; when candid camera shooting in the streets does not allow lighting, adjust the speed of the camera according to the amount of light available; if the continuity of different shots does not link up right for a sequence, try jump cuts; to solve the problem of color incontinuity, cover it up by developing the film in B/W... Tricks like that go on forever.

**From sight to sound, let's talk about your music. I think the use of Frank Zappa's I have Been in You in Happy Together is brilliant: first we hear it while Lai Yiu-Fai is night-cruising in the streets, and that song conjures a mixture of sentimentalism and eroticism; then the song reappears during the abattoir sequence and transcends the whole scene. It is if, while flirting with life, Lai Yiu-Fai has one night been promoted from the physical level to a metaphysical one.

**I find *I Have Been in You* deeply erotic. Did I tell you that one night Chris was drunk and out of love again, and we were sitting in my office, and listened to the song over thirty times? Though most of the time he was in the toilet   wether

slumbering or crying I never knew.

**Technically, Happy Together marks something new for your works. Before this, sound had habitually been something to rush off a couple of hours before sending the copy to the laboratory for development; but this time you actually spent over two weeks working on the Dolby Surround Sound. I was impressed.*

**Objectively, for this film, I got about four months for postproduction and that is a record. I had more time to work on things that I never had the the time for before. Subjectively, I really wanted to make the most out of the songs and music by Frank Zappa and Astor Piazzolla — two great musicians I consider to be Bad Boys of their own tradition. (Pause.) I always believe that film is really nothing but sight and sound; and music is part of the sound.

Your habit of spending weeks on developing and redeveloping the film to your desired effect, while leaving only hours for the soundtrack seems illogical to me.

*Granted, that is a technical problem involving my time allocation. But most of the time, during shooting, I already have a picture in mind, of how that scene will look on screen; and I instinctually know if that scene is going to be accompanied by music or not. Generally, I see the whole music structure before the editing is finished. So physically fitting the music into the soundtrack is more like the final necessary step to complete the picture. I am quite confident in my music sense.

I can remember when Days of Being Wild came out, everybody found the music mesmerizing. I guess I can say that, to most people, the memory of the film comes with a built-in soundtrack. In that sense, the film has overtaken the music's original identity — Always In My Heart has since been adopted by Days of Being Wild. Later on, when Pulp Fiction came along, Tarantino did the same with You Never Can Tell — people who have seen the film will never hear the song again without seeing the fingers of John Travolta dancing.

*With some films, you can do that — carry two CDs into the studio and voila, you get all you want for your soundtrack.

That was what you did with Days of Being Wild. And then you tried a different approach with Ashes of Time.

*I had a serious headache with *Ashes of Time*, trying to come up with something for the soundtrack, different types of music that would be complementary for different moods and yet united in spirit. In the end, I had to give up the idea and opt for something original.

Some people find the film's music disturbing. Maybe they find it too grungy. I always think of Ashes of Time *the film industry's answer to the grunge culture.*

*I am not sure about the "grunge" theory that you started. What I do know is that, at some point, I was ready to try something more sophisticated, something that has more taste, so to say; but I found that unsatisfactory. So Frankie Chan came in and did the music for me. Granted, if I were to do it myself, I wouldn't do it the way Frankie did, but when I saw the finished product, I could see why he did it like that. Take Sergio Leone for example, when we go to see his films, we find his music very loud, but we understand it is the only way to do it properly.

About TV. How are you influenced by TV?

*I grew up watching TV. I guess I really belong to the first TV generation. Lots of movies I watched on TV.

Shouldn't we classify that as a "movie influence"?

*Not necessarily. Without TV, I wouldn't have seen it. Our generation has an advantage: we were more creative, more ready to try out different things. New things come out like that. Now, TV has become very much run of the mill, you get assigned nothing but routine. When I was working at the TV station, their decision to shoot TV series with film affected me much. Acquainting myself with film at that time, I found the movie world within reach. When I was a kid, I always found making movies something beyond reach. I had lots of neighbors working within the industry, and I was hugely impressed.

Now, it is the turn of Hollywood to be within reach.

*No way.

How would you imagine Wong Kar-Wai working in Hollywood?

*I don't think I want to work in Hollywood. I mean, just for the experience, I don't mind trying things out. But I really cannot see myself becoming a Hollywood entity. First of all, what would I do in Hollywood?

Are you confident that Hong Kong can afford to keep you?

*I always think… (Pause.) Questions like this won't work, because… I am a very insecure person, I cannot sit here and tell you what my plans for the next two years are. I try my best.

**I have always associated your sunglasses with insecurity. So Hong Kong has managed to keep you for another two years, and you still have no plans to change bases, not to Hollywood or anywhere else?*

**Lots of things are very circumstantial. People have always been concerned if I would be able to make the same films after the handover of 1997, or if I would change my direction for a much wider Chinese market. My opinion is that I don't have a list of films that I want to make in the coming so many years, and so I can't tell people if there is going to be any change. One day, I might just decide to throw in the towel and turn myself into an idle man enjoying life, not necessarily because of the political climate.

**I find it very intriguing that, on the one hand, your tender side looks back in time with unashamed fondness, as if each stroke of the hand of the clock could be the cause of another catastrophe; while on the other hand, you make fierce attempts in your*

works to make sure that the form, the narrative are nothing but daring, challenging the audience, challenging our watching habits. And then these two forces, fighting inside you, come to a truce and agree to come out and face the world in perfect harmony.

**One cannot see these things oneself. Everything comes natural. You add all the ingredients up, and that becomes me.

53 ▶▶

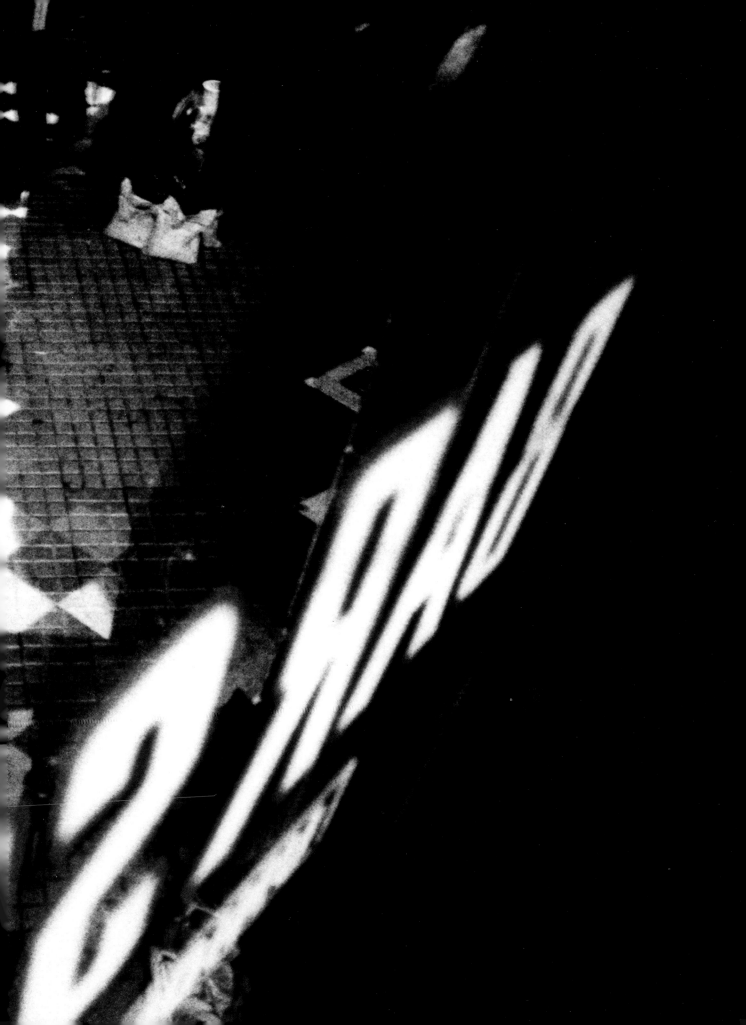

BIOGRAPHY

Director, Writer, Producer

Wong Kar-wai was born in Shanghai in 1958. He moved to Hong Kong with his parents at the age of five and graduated in graphic design from Hong Kong Polytechnic in 1980. He then enrolled in the television station TVB's Production Training Course and soon began working as a production assistant on drama serials. He left TVB in 1982 to become a full-time script-writer for feature films. Over the following five years he wrote some ten feature scripts, ranging in genre from romantic comedies to action dramas. Of these, he considered *Final Victory* (1986, directed by Patrick Tam) his best script.

Wong directed his own first feature *As Tears Go By* in 1988. The script bore a heavy debt to Martin Scorcese's Mean Streets, but the strong visual style was entirely Wong's own. The film was nominated in ten categories at the Hong Kong Film Awards and was invited to the Critic Week section of the 1989 Cannes Film Festival.

In 1990 Wong assembled a cast of the most popular young actors in Hong Kong and made *Days of Being Wild*, a nostalgic epic set in the 1960's and originally intended to be in two parts. The film won five Hong Kong Film Awards, including Best Film, Best Director and Best Actor (for Leslie Cheung), but its disappointing box-office returns meant that the planned second part had to be aborted. The film has since been released with considerable success in Japan, the UK and other countries.

In 1992 assembled another cast of Hong Kong's top stars for *Ashes of Time*, a martial arts drama shot in remote regions of China. The film was nearly two years in production. It won a Best Cinematography at the 1994 Venice Film Festival.

Chungking Express, Wong's biggest international hit to date, was made incredibly quickly during a two-month break in the post-production of *Ashes of Time*. Some of the film's principal locations in Hong Kong have become sites of pilgrimage for fans (especially from Japan), and the film's world-wide success has prompted the opening of a Hong Kong shop devoted to memorabilia from Wong Kar-wai's films.

Fallen Angels (1995) was developed from storylines originally intended for *Chungking Express*. Shot entirely through wide-angle lenses, it is in many ways Wong's most daring and experimental film.

Happy Together was almost entirely shot on locations in Argentina (Buenos Aires, Patagonia and Mendoza) in the second half of 1996. Brief additionnal scenes were shot in Taipei and Hong Kong in the early months of 1997. The film won the Prix de la Mise en Scène at the 1997 Cannes Festival.

FILMOGRAPHY

Scripts (selection)

1980 *Don't look now (série TV)*
1982 *Once upon a rainbow*
1985 *Chase a fortune*
1987 *Final Victory*, Patrick Tam
1988 *Haunted Cop Shop 2,* Yuen Cheung Yan
1991 *Saviour of the Soul*, Corey Yuen/David Lai (not credited)
1992 *92'Legendary La Rose Noire*, Jeff Lau (not credited)
1995 *A Chinese Odissey*, Jeff Lau (co-writer, not credited)

Director

1988 AS TEARS GO BY

> *Script Writer*: Wong Kar-wai
> *Producer*: Rover Tang
> *Executive Producer*: Alan Tang
> *Director of Photography*: Andrew Lau
> *Production Designer*: William Chang Suk-ping
> *Editor*: Peter Chiang
> *Music*: Danny Chung
> *Starring*: Andy Lau Tak-wah, Maggie Cheung Man-yuk, Jackie Cheung Hok-yau, Alex Man

1991 DAYS OF BEING WILD

> *Script Writer*: Wong Kar-wai
> *Producer*: Rover Tang
> *Executive Producer*: Alan Tang
> *Director of Photography*: Chris Doyle
> *Production Designer*: William Chang Suk-ping
> *Editor*: Kai Kit-wai, Patrick Tam Kar-ming
> *Music*: Xavier Cugat, Django Reinhardt
> *Starring*: Leslie Cheung Kwok-wing, Maggie Cheung Man-yuk, Andy Lau Tak-wah, Jackie Cheung Hok-yau, Carinau Lau Kar-ling, Tony Leung Chiu-wai.

1994 ASHES OF TIME

Script Writer: Wong Kar-wai
Producer: Tsai Mu-ho
Executive Producer: Shu Kei
Director of Photography: Chris Doyle
Production Designer: William Chang
Suk-ping
Choreography: Samo Hung Kam-bo
Editor: William Chang Suk-ping, Kai
Kit-wai, Patrick Tam Kar-ming, Kwong
Chi-leung
Music: Frankie Chan & Roel A. Garcia
Starring: Leslie Cheung Kwok-wing,
Tony Leung Kar-fai, Charlie Yeung Cho-
nei, Jackie Cheung Hok-yau, Carinau
Lau Kar-ling.

1994 CHUNGKING EXPRESS

Script Writer: Wong Kar-wai
Producer: Chan Ye-Cheng
Executive Producer: Wong Kar-wai
Director of Photography: Chris Doyle
Production Designer: William Chang
Suk-ping
Editor: William Chang Suk-ping, Kai
Kit-wai, Kwong Chi-leung
Music: Frankie Chan & Roel A. Garcia
Starring: Faye Wong, Brigitte Lin Ching-
hsia, Tony Leung Chiu-wai, Takeshi
Kaneshiro, Valerie Chow Kar-ling.

1995 FALLEN ANGELS

Script Writer: Wong Kar-wai
Producer: Jeff Lau
Executive Producer: Jacky Pang Yee-wah
Director of Photography: Chris Doyle
Production Designer: William Chang
Suk-ping
Editor: William Chang Suk-ping, Wong
Ming-lam
Music: Frankie Chan & Roel A. Garcia
Starring: Leon Lai-ming, Michelle Li Ka-
yan, Takeshi Kaneshiro, Karen Mok
Man-wai, Charlie Yeung Choi-nei.

1997 HAPPY TOGETHER

Script Writer: Wong Kar-wai
Producer: Wong Kar-wai
Executive Producer: Chan Ye-Cheng
Director of Photography: Chris Doyle
Production Designer: William Chang
Suk-ping
Editor: William Chang Suk-ping, Wong
Ming-lam
Music: Dany Chung
Starring: Leslie Cheung Kwok-wing, Tony
Leung Chiu-wai, Chang Chen.

29 *Happy Together*
30 *Chungking Express*
31 *Happy Together*
32 *Happy Together*
33 *Fallen Angels*
34 *Fallen Angels*
35 *Happy Together*
36 *Fallen Angels*
37 *Happy Together*
38 *Happy Together*
39 *Happy Together*
40 *Chungking Express*
41 *Ashes of Time*
42 *Happy Together*
43 *Happy Together*
44 *Happy Together*
45 *Ashes of Time*
46 *Ashes of Time*
47 *Ashes of Time*
48 *Happy Together*
49 *Happy Together*
50 *Chungking Express*
51 *Happy Together*
52 *Happy Together*
53 *Happy Together*
54 *Chungking Express*
55 *Fallen Angels*
56 *Chungking Express* (on the stage)

Also available from Dis Voir

PLASTIC ARTS

François Dagognet
In Favour of Today's Art

Jean-Yves Bosseur
Sound and the Visual Arts

Thierry de Duve
Clement Greenberg between the lines

Alain Charre, Marie-Paule MacDonald, Marc Perelman
Dan Graham

Gertrud Koch, Luc Lang, Jean-Philippe Antoine
Gerhard Richter

Christine Savinel, Jacques Roubaud, Bernard Noël
Roman Opalka

Christine Macel, Marc Perelman, Jacinto Lageira
Jean-Marc Bustamante

Jeff Wall, Ludger Gerdes, Hervé Vanel, Ingrid Schaffner
Stephan Balkenhol

LITERATURE/FINE ART/CINEMA

Raúl Ruiz
Poetics of Cinema
The Book of Disappearances & The Book of Tractations
A la Poursuite de l'Ile au Trésor

Peter Greenaway
The Falls
Rosa
Fear of Drowning by Numbers
Papers - (Paintings, Collages and Drawings)
The Cook, the Thief, his Wife and her Lover
The Baby of Mâcon
The Pillow Book

Manoel de Oliveira
Les Cannibales

CINEMA

Jean-Marc Lalanne, Ackbar Abbas, David Martinez, Jimmy Ngai
Wong Kar-wai

Paul Virilio, Carole Desbarats, Jacinto Lageira, Danièle Rivière
Atom Egoyan

Michael Nyman, Daniel Caux, Michel Field, Florence de Mèredieu, Philippe Pilard
Peter Greenaway

Christine Buci-Glucksmann, Fabrice Revault d'Allonnes
Raúl Ruiz

Yann Lardeau, Jacques Parsi, Philippe Tancelin
Manoel de Oliveira

CHOREOGRAPHY

Paul Virilio, René Thom, Laurence Louppe, Jean-Noël Laurenti, Valérie Preston-Dunlop
Traces of Dance - Drawings and Notations of Choreographers

ARCHITECTURE

Christian de Portzamparc
Genealogy of forms

DESIGN

Raymond Guidot, Olivier Boissière
Ron Arad

François Burkhardt, Cristina Morozzi
Andrea Branzi

ÉDITIONS DIS VOIR: 3, RUE BEAUTREILLIS - F-75004 PARIS
PHONE (33 - 1) 48 87 07 09 - FAX (33 - 1) 48 87 07 14

128